Assassination!

KENNEDY, KING, KENNEDY

Assassination!

KENNEDY, KING, KENNEDY

by Stephen Goode

FRANKLIN WATTS | NEW YORK | LONDON | 1979

Photographs courtesy of:

Fabian Bachrach: p. 4; United Press International:
pp. 9, 17, 25 (left and right), 73, 74, 79, 86, 92, 95,
96, 101, 134, 144, 149, 156; Wide World Photos: pp.
10, 24, 32, 108, 119; Wilma I. Bond: p. 14 (top and
bottom).

Art by Rod Slater

Library of Congress Cataloging in Publication Data

Goode, Stephen.
Assassination! Kennedy, King, Kennedy.

Bibliography: p.
Includes index.
SUMMARY: Discusses the assassinations of President Kennedy, Martin Luther King, Jr., and Robert
Kennedy, the investigations of the murders, and the
lingering suspicions that these crimes are still un-
solved.
1. Kennedy, John Fitzgerald, Pres. U.S., 1917–
1963—Assassination—Juvenile literature. 2. Kennedy, Robert F., 1925–1968—Assassination—Juvenile literature. 3. King, Martin Luther—Assassination—Juvenile literature. [1. Kennedy, John
Fitzgerald, Pres. U.S., 1917–1963—Assassination. 2.
Kennedy, Robert F., 1925–1968—Assassination. 3.
King, Martin Luther—Assassination. 4. Assassina-
tions] I. Title.
E842.9.G59   973.92   78–10227
ISBN 0-531-02213-7

FOR JODY AND
AIMEE BUSCHMAN

Contents

Assassination!

KENNEDY, KING, KENNEDY

Preface

This is a book about one facet of a particularly violent and tumultuous period of American history, the 1960s. Its subject is the assassination of three prominent and respected Americans, President John Fitzgerald Kennedy, Dr. Martin Luther King, Jr., and Senator Robert Francis Kennedy. But this book is about much more than the assassinations themselves. It is also about the investigations that followed the murders of these three famous men and about the widespread belief that the investigations were inadequate and did not uncover the whole truth.

The subject is deeply controversial. The assassinations have been the theme of numerous books and magazine articles. Television and radio have likewise looked into the matter. The outcome has been a wide variety of opinion and speculation. Reasonable men and women have come to different conclusions using the same evidence and information. Some believe the facts point in one direction; others are not so sure and believe we should look in another. Frequently the debate has degenerated into heated argument, name-calling, and worse. Proponents of one side accuse the other of distortion, misrepresentation, and outright lying. The other side answers with the same condemnations.

This book will come to no final conclusions about the assassinations. Rather, it will survey the material and arguments that have been put forth by a variety of people and show that important issues have been raised by men and women with widely differing views. Hopefully the reader will come to some conclusions of his or her own.

One note of warning should be sounded before we begin. The most difficult problem with cases such as these is that in the American legal system, guilt must be proved beyond a shadow of reasonable doubt. Gossip and speculation do not stand up in court, only solid evidence and "cold" facts. With this severe test in mind, the reader is invited to imagine that he or she has been chosen to sit on a jury that will decide the guilt or innocence of those accused of these crimes. The good juror will be impartial and objective—and weigh carefully both the strong and the weak points in the case. The bad juror will "rush to judgment," and make his or her decision on the basis of emotion, sentiment, or vague feelings.

Section One

The Assassination of John Fitzgerald Kennedy

JOHN FITZGERALD KENNEDY, 1917–1963

Chapter One

NOVEMBER 22, 1963:
DALLAS, TEXAS

In November 1960, John Fitzgerald Kennedy was elected the thirty-fifth President of the United States. Handsome, youthful, and charismatic, he presented a striking contrast to the outgoing President, Dwight David Eisenhower, who was twenty-six years his senior. Eisenhower had inspired confidence and a sense of security; Kennedy promised change and innovation. Many Americans looked with hope toward the new Administration. They believed that a new and dynamic President might well improve conditions at home, as well as establish better relations with peoples throughout the world.

But Kennedy had won the 1960 election by only 118,574 votes out of the almost 69 million cast. This narrow victory limited his influence over Congress and made passage of much of his legislation difficult. During his first years in office, Kennedy was unable to deliver on his campaign promises. Some observers predicted that he would be a one-term President, rejected by his own party if he attempted to run for the office again. Kennedy, however, seemed to relish the Presidency and, after a few initial mistakes, began to mature in it. His intelligence and courage impressed increasing numbers of people, but perhaps most striking was the Kennedy style, a combination of wit, optimism, and ability, which many Americans found captivating and exciting.

As his popularity began to grow, President Kennedy determined that he would win the next presidential election by the largest possible margin. A decisive victory would give him the mandate he needed to carry out his plans for the country, and it would force the men and women in Congress to follow his leadership. With this in mind, Kennedy began to campaign for the 1964 elections more than a year before they were to occur.

Central to Kennedy's campaign strategy was the state of Texas. Texas was large and populous, with an important twenty-four electoral votes. In 1960, he had carried the state largely due to the efforts of his vice-presidential candidate, Lyndon Johnson, who was himself a Texan. But conditions had changed since 1960, and the Democratic party in Texas had fallen on bad times. The party was now bitterly divided between a liberal wing, headed by Senator Ralph Yarborough, and a conservative wing, led by Governor John Connally. The dispute between the two men had grown so bitter that they did not speak to each other. It threatened to undermine the power of the party in a state traditionally Democratic and lead to a Republican victory at the polls.

Kennedy hoped that a presidential visit to Texas might help to heal the rift between the two men. For more than a year there had been talk of such a visit, but plans were not definitely set until June 1963. At that time it was decided that the President would make his tour of the state in late November. Speaking engagements were set up for the major cities—San Antonio, Houston, Fort Worth, and Dallas. In addition, it was proposed that Kennedy would ride in a motorcade in each city, so that he would be seen by as many Texans as possible.

Perhaps the single most important stop the President would make was Dallas. No Texas city was more bitterly divided. Dallas was the home of several outspoken right-wing groups that were strongly opposed to Kennedy and his policies. Only one week before his scheduled visit, several Dallas extremists verbally abused Adlai Stevenson, who had come to the city to deliver a speech. Stevenson was the American ambassador to the United Nations and a former Democratic candidate for President. Some demonstrators had spat on him and at least one struck him on the head with a placard.

The incident had disturbed Stevenson so much that he felt compelled to warn the President about Dallas and to suggest that he cancel his trip there. But Kennedy did not take the advice. He considered Dallas central to his campaign plans for Texas and did not see how he could avoid his obligations there. Besides, Kennedy had frequently commented that no amount of protection could defend him from someone determined to do him harm. He could as easily be killed in Washington, D.C., as in Dallas.

Kennedy and his wife, Jacqueline, arrived in Texas on Thursday, November 21. Almost everywhere they went the crowds were large, warm, and enthusiastic. They spent the night in Fort Worth, encouraged and hopeful; the visit really seemed to be healing the split in the party. But the President's spirit sagged as he read the *Dallas Morning News* the next morning. A full-page advertisement denounced him as a traitor and a Communist, a man unfit to be the President of the United States. The ad further called for his removal from office and declared that his presence in Dallas was unwelcome. Kennedy was angered and bewildered by the attack and remarked to some of his aides that he could not understand such bitterness. What kind of hatred, he asked, could lead people to call him a Communist and a traitor, when he was so obviously neither?

A little after 11:30 a.m., the presidential plane, *Air Force One,* landed at Love Field outside of Dallas. For the most part, the crowd at the airport was friendly and warm. Kennedy and his wife stopped to mingle and shake hands. From the time he had first run for Congress from his district in Massachusetts, Kennedy had firmly believed in the importance of close personal contact. He enjoyed crowds, and they enjoyed him.

Kennedy was scheduled to address an assembly of the city's notables at the new Trade Mart. A motorcade was planned to take him through the heart of Dallas, where he could be seen by the people. A pilot car led the parade, followed by a car with Dallas Police Chief Jesse Curry. Then came the presidential limousine, with the President and his wife and Governor and Mrs. Connally. Other limousines carried Vice-President Johnson and his wife, Senator Yarborough, and various state and local dignitaries. There was also a car filled with Secret Service agents—men carefully selected to protect the President—immediately following the presidential limousine.

Not far from its final destination, the Trade Mart, the motorcade passed through Dealey Plaza, named for the founder of the *Dallas Morning News.* Here several of the city's main streets came together to form one. That street then ran under a railway overpass and joined Stemmons Freeway. Dealey Plaza was the last place the public would be able to see Kennedy and his wife up close. As it neared Stemmons Freeway, the motor-

THIS PICTURE OF THE PRESIDENT AND HIS WIFE
WAS TAKEN JUST MOMENTS BEFORE THE SHOOTING.
GOVERNOR CONNALLY AND HIS WIFE ARE IN
THE SEATS JUST IN FRONT OF THE KENNEDYS.

PRESIDENT KENNEDY CAN BE SEEN
SLUMPING INTO THE ARMS OF HIS WIFE AS HE IS
HIT BY ONE OF THE ASSASSIN'S BULLETS.

cade would speed up in order to reach the Trade Mart in time for the President's speaking engagement.

Near Dealey Plaza there were several tall buildings, including one known as the Texas School Book Depository. Moments before the motorcade arrived, some people in the crowd lining the street opposite noticed figures in a window on the sixth floor of the Depository. Mrs. Carolyn Walther later testified that she saw two men—one of whom held a rifle—but assumed that the men were placed there to guard the President. Another witness saw only one man in the window, but noticed that the rifle had telescopic sights.

As the motorcade approached the plaza, the presidential limousine slowed down to make a sharp turn. Only a few more minutes and the ride would be over. Mrs. Kennedy and Mrs. Connally both breathed a sigh of relief. Then suddenly and without warning, several shots rang out. To some the shots sounded like firecrackers exploding—perhaps to celebrate the President's visit. Others, however, immediately recognized what was happening and fell to the ground to protect themselves.

The spectacle witnessed by many of the people in Dealey Plaza was terrifying. First, they could see the President's face register pain. Then, perhaps a split second later, they saw his head react to a second bullet, one that tore through the back of his skull and sent fragments of bone, blood, and brains scattering over his wife, Mrs. Connally, and the limousine. At the same time, Governor Connally collapsed in his wife's arms in great pain.

Out of the chaos that followed came many conflicting reports. Some witnesses were certain that three shots had been fired, others were equally certain they had heard four. Some were convinced that the shots had come from the overpass in front of the limousine, while a number of others believed they had come from a grassy knoll in front and to the right of the President's car.

Dallas policemen fanned out in both directions. Dallas Police Chief Jesse Curry, who had been in the lead car of the motorcade, thought the shots had come from the overpass. He grabbed a microphone and ordered some of his men to get to the spot as quickly as possible. At the same time, Bobby Hargis, a motorcycle policeman who was near the President when the shots rang out, abandoned his motorcycle and ran toward the grassy knoll. In neither place, however, was there evidence that a rifle had been fired—no spent cartridge shells, no one carrying a weapon.

A third group of witnesses believed the shots had come from the School Book Depository. This group included several people from the crowd in Dealey Plaza who looked up at the sixth-floor Depository window right after the shots were fired and saw a rifle. Also among these witnesses were three Depository employees who were watching the motorcade from the fifth floor, just below the spot where the shots seemed to have come from.

One of the employees on the fifth floor, Harold Norman, later claimed that he and his companions had heard what sounded like a shell casing drop on the floor above them, right after they saw Kennedy being shot. When a second shot was fired, Norman this time heard the explosion and noticed that a fine white powder settled on the head and shoulders of one of his friends— plaster from the ceiling that had shaken loose as the rifle above was fired.

Marrion Baker was the first policeman to reach the Depository. Baker promptly located the building man-

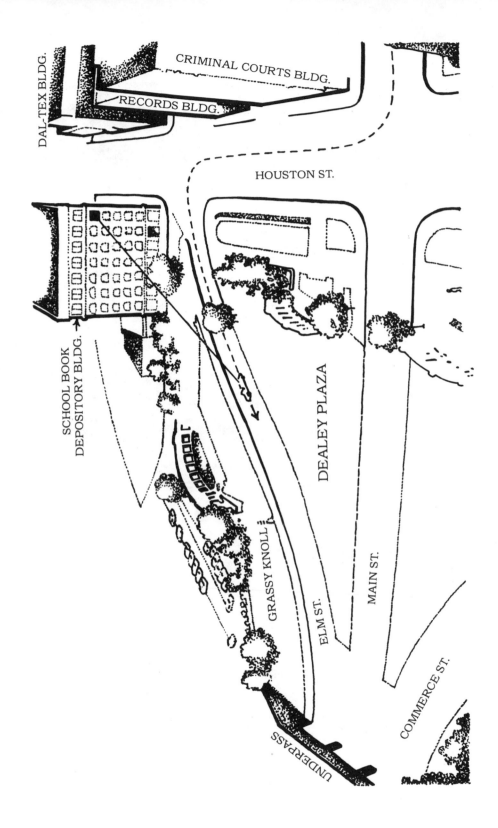

AFTER THE SHOOTING, HARGIS (ARROW IN BOTH
PHOTOS) STOPPED, GOT OFF HIS MOTORCYCLE, AND
LED THE CHASE UP THE GRASSY KNOLL. LATER,
HE TOLD THE COMMISSION THAT HE THOUGHT A
SHOT HAD COME FROM THAT DIRECTION.

ager, and together the two men began to search. On the second floor, they encountered a young man in a white shirt, sipping a Coke. Baker began to question the man, but stopped when the building manager told him that the young man worked in the Depository and was not a suspicious character.

Soon other policemen arrived and joined in the search, which quickly began to bear fruit. On the sixth floor, behind some packing cases, they found three shell casings on the floor. On the opposite side of the same room, they found a rifle with telescopic sights. The School Book Depository was sealed to protect the evidence and to prevent people from leaving or entering the building. The police also began to question employees, in an effort to discover who might have had access to the sixth floor.

Meanwhile, the presidential limousine left Dealey Plaza and headed for Parkland Memorial Hospital. A team of doctors was rushed together to care for the wounded President, but they held little hope for his recovery. The head wound was too serious. A second wound, the seriousness of which could not be judged immediately, was discovered in the President's neck. The doctors performed a tracheotomy to help him breathe more easily and began other efforts to relieve his condition. But all to no avail. A priest was summoned to perform last rites, and at 1:00 p.m., Central Standard Time—about one half hour after he had been shot—John Kennedy was officially declared dead.

At about the same time the President died, the man spotted by Marrion Baker casually sipping a Coke in the Depository after the assassination arrived at the room he rented in another part of Dallas. The man had rented the room under the name O. H. Lee. After finishing his drink, he had left work for the day, caught a bus, abandoned it when it had become snarled in traffic, and then completed his trip by cab. Now he rushed into his room, tucked a .38-calibre revolver under his belt, put on a dark jacket—probably to hide the gun—and left without speaking to anyone, not even his landlady, Earlene Roberts, who saw him enter and depart.

A few minutes later, several blocks from Lee's boardinghouse, a young police officer, J. D. Tippit, was cruising the area in his police car. A little after 1:00 p.m., Tippit stopped his car on East Tenth Street, evidently to question a man he thought suspicious. The man drew a gun and shot Tippit four times before turning and running away. Bystanders quickly summoned other policemen and rushed to the aid of the wounded officer, only to discover that he was already dead. Later, the witnesses disagreed strongly on what they had seen. One believed Tippit had stopped two men, one short, the other tall. The shorter man had drawn and fired the gun. Others said the gunman had been alone, but their descriptions of his physical appearance and clothing varied.

On West Jefferson Boulevard, not far from the scene of Tippit's murder, Johnny Brewer, the manager of a shoe store, heard on his radio that a police officer had been killed nearby. Almost at the same time he heard the news report, Brewer looked up to see a man duck into the doorway of his store, as if to avoid being seen by passing police cars. His suspicions aroused, Brewer began to follow the man and saw him enter a nearby movie theatre without paying. He told the ticket-taker about the unpaid customer and then went inside.

The ticket-taker called the police, who arrived a short time later. Some covered the exits; others followed Brewer inside. The houselights were turned on and the film brought to a stop. About fifteen people sat in the

POLICE OFFICER J. D. TIPPIT,
SECOND VICTIM OF LEE HARVEY OSWALD?

lower level of the movie house. At first, the police had no idea which one of the fifteen they were looking for, but then someone in the theatre turned to officer N. M. McDonald and told him that the man the police wanted was sitting three rows from the back, near the middle. The identity of this informant has remained a mystery.

McDonald slowly made his way to the back, searching the audience as he went, yet all the while keeping an eye on the man he had been warned about. When McDonald reached the back rows, the man stood up and said, "It's all over now." McDonald tried to grab him, but the man struck him hard on the face and drew a gun. Other policemen soon joined in the struggle and eventually they brought the suspect under control.

At first, the police connected the arrested man primarily with the murder of J. D. Tippit. After questioning him, however, they believed they had reason to charge him with much more. First, the police discovered that the man carried two different identification cards. One bore the name Alek Hiddell, which proved to be fictitious; the second was under the name Lee Harvey Oswald. The police had already come across that name once that day. It had been included on a list of Texas School Book Depository employees who had failed to return to work after Kennedy's assassination. The question arose now as to whether the suspect had been involved in the murder of President Kennedy as well as that of Officer Tippit.

Lee Harvey Oswald remained calm and collected under cross-examination. He told the police that he was familiar with their methods of interrogation, since he had been questioned on several occasions by the FBI. He said he had been eating lunch at the Depository with a man named "Junior" when the President was shot. He also acknowledged that he had been sipping a

Coke when Officer Baker passed him on the second floor. He had left work, he added, simply because he thought the assassination would bring things to a standstill and the Depository would be closed off.

Oswald said that his Russian wife, Marina, and their two children lived in the Dallas suburb of Irving with a Mrs. Ruth Paine. Mrs. Paine provided a place for them to live in exchange for Russian lessons. He was able to visit his family only on weekends. During the week, he lived in the city. Oswald admitted that he had lived in the Soviet Union and that he considered himself a Marxist. But he said that he had no hatred for President Kennedy or for the Kennedy family. He denied owning a rifle and he refused to accept any responsibility for the assassination of the President or for the murder of Tippit. His only crime, he claimed, was striking the police officer who arrested him.

Around 3:00 that afternoon, police detectives arrived in Irving to question Marina Oswald. Mrs. Oswald told them in Russian—her English was poor and Mrs. Paine acted as translator—that her husband did indeed own a rifle and that he kept it in the garage. When the detectives looked for the weapon, however, they discovered that it was missing; only an empty, oil-stained blanket gave any hint that it may have been where Marina said it was.

In the room Oswald and his wife shared, the police discovered several personal papers, including Communist tracts and pamphlets that supported Fidel Castro. They also discovered Oswald's wedding band, which he had evidently removed from his finger that morning. Marina had failed to notice it earlier. Now she was shocked and dismayed. She and her husband had not been happily married for some time, she said, and the removed ring seemed to indicate that he had made a final decision to break with her that morning. The detectives found it significant that Oswald had spent the previous night in Irving with his wife. For some reason, he had broken his usual pattern of visiting the family only on weekends. Had he bothered to come to his wife on Thursday because he knew that on Friday he might be arrested for the assassination?

The police then questioned Wesley Frazier, a young man who lived a few doors from Mrs. Paine and had given Oswald a ride to work that morning. Frazier told them that Oswald had carried a long, narrow package with him and when asked what the package contained, had replied, "Curtain rods." The curtain rods were for his furnished room in Dallas, he had added. Frazier's sister likewise told police that she had seen the package.

As the police began to piece their case together, they were encouraged by the testimony of several witnesses who could link Oswald with the murders of President Kennedy and Tippit. Oswald fit the description of the man in the sixth-story window of the Depository offered by Howard Brennan, a man who had been in the plaza below when the shots were fired. Brennan's eyesight was not good and his testimony would waver over the next few months, but on November 22 the police believed they could use what he had to say as evidence against the man they had arrested in the movie house. In addition, Oswald could be placed at the scene of Tippit's murder by witnesses who had seen him running away shortly after the shots were fired. These witnesses were able to identify Oswald in a police lineup.

Encouraging, too, was Oswald's own testimony. Even though he had remained calm under questioning, the police realized they had caught Oswald in several lies. He had claimed that he did not own a rifle, when, in fact, he did own one. He denied carrying a package to work that morning, when, in fact, two reliable witnesses had seen him carrying one. He had told one of the witnesses that the package contained curtain rods for his furnished room, but when the police questioned Earlene Roberts, Oswald's Dallas landlady, they learned that the room did not need curtain rods. Even if the room had needed them, Mrs. Roberts added, she would not have allowed him to put them up.

Oswald was arraigned for the Tippit murder at 7:10 p.m. and at 1:30 early the next morning for the Kennedy assassination. Around midnight of November 22, the police allowed reporters to interview their suspect. The room where the conference was held was hot and crowded. Many of the newspeople present were visibly angered by the assassination and unsympathetic to the man accused of the crime. But Oswald held his ground. He denied killing Kennedy and he denied killing Tippit. He complained that the police had not allowed him to find adequate legal representation and that he had been struck by a policeman during his capture. He did not mention, as he had in previous questioning, that he himself had struck first and had even drawn a gun to threaten the officer.

Very early on the Dallas police somewhat grudgingly agreed to cooperate with the FBI in investigating the assassination, even though they considered the crime to be a local matter. They knew that they alone did not have the staff and equipment to conduct a full investigation. Clues were coming in that connected Oswald with New Orleans and Mexico City, not to mention the Soviet Union. Only the FBI had the ability to follow the entire case. So it was decided that the evidence gathered in Dallas—the rifle, the revolver, the contents of Oswald's room, and so on—would be listed, examined, photographed, and then sent to Washington to the FBI laboratories. For its part, the FBI agreed to keep the evidence available to the Dallas police for Oswald's trial.

About 6:00 p.m., as Oswald was being questioned at police headquarters, President Kennedy's body arrived in Washington, D.C. An official autopsy was performed at the National Naval Medical Center in Bethesda, Maryland. The doctors there determined that his death had been due to the bullet that struck the back of his head. After the autopsy, the body was prepared for burial and taken to lie in state in the Capitol rotunda. More than 250,000 people stood in line to file past the coffin and pay their last respects. On November 25, Kennedy was taken to St. Matthew's Cathedral, where a requiem mass was held. Afterward, he was buried in Arlington Cemetery in a plot that had been prepared for him when news of his death reached Washington.

The frightening and tragic events in Dallas did not come to an end with Oswald's capture and arrest. For two days the police kept the suspect in the city jail and questioned him repeatedly about the assassination. On Saturday, they announced that they were going to transfer him to the county jail the next day for security reasons; already the Dallas FBI headquarters and the sheriff's office had received threats against Oswald's life. This also was standard procedure: every person charged with a felony in Dallas is handed over to the county sheriff for custody and Oswald was no exception.

On Sunday, November 24, Oswald was taken from his cell. The police had worked out a decoy plan whereby a truck parked near the exit to the city jail would drive away about the time Oswald was scheduled to leave. In that way, any potential assassin would think that the prisoner had already left, giving the police time to take him away secretly in a police car.

With two detectives on either side, Oswald was forced to make his way through a crowd of people the police had not carefully screened. Television cameras, taking the scene to an estimated twenty million viewers, were trained on him. Suddenly, a short, heavyset man dressed in a suit and hat stepped out of the crowd, brandishing a .38 revolver. At the last minute, Oswald seemed to realize what was taking place. He raised his hands to protect himself, but without success. He was shot once at close range and died two hours later.

The man who had fired the gun was Jack Ruby, a well-known Dallas nightclub owner. Ruby later told police that he had been deeply angered by President Kennedy's assassination. He said his grief had caused him to be the only nightclub owner in Dallas to close his club that evening out of respect for the late President. For two days, he added, he had thought about the crime, and about how horrible it was that it had happened in Dallas. Months later, Ruby changed his story, claiming instead that he had killed Oswald because he did not want the President's widow to have to return to Dallas to testify at a trial. She had suffered enough, he believed, and should be spared any further discomfort.

Ruby's act opened up a Pandora's box of unanswered questions and speculations that are still very much with us today. Oswald had maintained to the end his absolute innocence and had claimed that, given time, he could prove that he was not guilty. Now he would not have that time. Already there were many people throughout the world who were wondering if he had been killed to keep him from revealing the names of accomplices. Many others wondered if he were guilty at all—if, in fact, the Dallas police had seized the wrong man. Oswald alive may never have answered all questions to everyone's satisfaction, but Oswald dead could answer no questions at all.

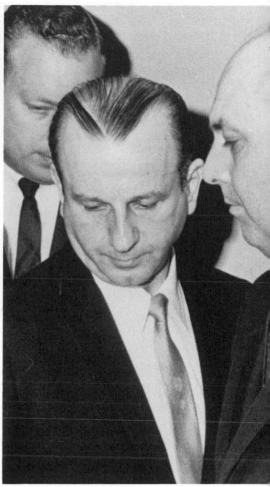

OPPOSITE: OSWALD IS SHOT TO DEATH BY
JACK RUBY, A NEW ORLEANS NIGHTCLUB
OWNER, IN FRONT OF MILLIONS OF
ASTONISHED TELEVISION VIEWERS.
ABOVE LEFT: MARINA OSWALD WEEPS AT
THE GRAVESITE SERVICES FOR HER
HUSBAND. ABOVE RIGHT: JACK RUBY, WHO
DIED IN PRISON OF CANCER IN JANUARY
1967. RUBY HAD SERVED ONLY A SMALL
PART OF HIS TERM FOR KILLING OSWALD,
AND THE TRUTH ABOUT WHY HE DID IT
MAY HAVE BEEN BURIED WITH HIM.

Chapter Two

THE OFFICIAL INVESTIGATION

The assassination of John Kennedy shocked the nation and the world. It was the first successful attempt against the life of an American President in more than sixty years. Americans reacted with hurt and anger over the loss of their vigorous and respected leader. Many Americans also feared that the assassination was a sign of an increasingly troubled and disturbed American society.

Moreover, the events in Dallas suggested that there was more to the assassination than met the eye. Had Oswald acted alone? Had he been in the pay of a foreign country or of Americans who wished to see Kennedy dead? These and other questions had to be answered. To let them go unresolved would invite all sorts of hearsay and dangerous gossip, which might undermine the effectiveness of the government or further damage the American image abroad.

One of those most concerned about clearing up the mystery surrounding the assassination was Lyndon Johnson, the new President of the United States. In the days after Kennedy's death, Johnson voiced his anxiety to some of his associates. He said he feared that uninhibited speculation about the assassination could embroil the United States in a war where millions would lose their lives—particularly if that speculation involved the Soviet Union or Castro's Cuba. He believed the best way to lay these fears to rest was the establishment of a "blue-ribbon panel," composed of highly respected and trustworthy individuals, which would look into the matter and issue a report.

With this in mind, Johnson went to Earl Warren, the Chief Justice of the Supreme Court, and asked him to head the panel. Warren at first declined, pointing out that he was a highly unpopular figure in many parts of the country. Any committee he chaired, he felt, might come under severe criticism, and the President's efforts to calm the fears stemming from the assassination would fail. But Johnson insisted, and at last Warren accepted the task.

Johnson appointed six other men of national reputation to sit on the panel with Warren. Two came from the Senate, two from the House of Representatives, and two from among those who had public careers outside of politics. The senators were Richard Russell, a Democrat from Georgia, considered by many to be the most powerful member of Congress, and John Sherman Cooper, a Republican from Kentucky. The representatives were Hale Boggs, a Democrat from Louisiana, and Gerald Ford, a Republican from Michigan, both highly influential members of their respective parties. The others were Allen Dulles, the former head of the CIA, and John McCloy, who had been a special disarmament advisor during the Kennedy Administration.

At the first executive session of the panel which came to be known as the Warren Commission, Warren tried to impress his associates with the gravity of their assignment. He told them about President Johnson's fears concerning the stories that were circulating throughout the world. It was of utmost importance, he said, that the commission settle all problems related to the assassination, so that the nation could get on with business as usual.

Since the commissioners were themselves busy men, most of the investigative work became the responsibility of the commission staff—a group of talented, intelligent, and ambitious lawyers. The staff was under the directorship of J. Lee Rankin, a New York attorney who had served as Solicitor General of the United States. Others on the staff included William Coleman, the only black member, Albert Jenner, David Belin, and Arlen Specter. Each of these men would in later years gain substantial reputations in politics or public service.

To facilitate its work, the staff was broken down into separate teams. Each team was to devote its time and effort to one phase of the investigation. One team, for instance, would handle all the basic facts of the assassination. Another would work on Oswald's background and possible motives, while a third would concentrate on the autopsy material, and so on. Early in the investigation, the members of the commission decided to rely on the evidence supplied by the FBI and CIA, since the commission itself did not have the time, money, nor the staff of experts needed to examine the data scientifically.

On September 28, 1964, after almost nine months of work, the commission submitted its report to President Johnson and to the nation. The report was an overnight bestseller. Its first printing was sold out within twenty-four hours of publication and a second printing sold just as quickly. Even the twenty-six volumes of supporting material sold surprisingly well, for the most part to libraries and to private citizens who wanted to look over the findings of the commission.

The initial reaction to the report was positive. Many

people accepted it as final and conclusive. Newspaper editors praised the commission for the hard and thorough work it had done. "The quest for truth in the Kennedy assassination has been long and arduous," wrote Harrison Salisbury, a widely known and influential reporter for *The New York Times*. But now, he concluded, "no material question . . . remains unresolved so far as the death of President Kennedy is concerned."

What had the Warren Commission Report concluded about the assassination? First, it stated that "persuasive" evidence existed which showed that Lee Harvey Oswald had been the assassin. But more importantly, the report went on to say, Oswald had acted alone. There was no evidence of conspiracy, no evidence that Oswald had had outside help or encouragement of any kind. Jack Ruby had not been an accomplice, and he had not killed Oswald to silence him. Ruby had acted impulsively, after spending two days angrily reflecting on the assassination.

For many on the commission staff, the key to the assassination was the murder of Officer J. D. Tippit. Oswald, they believed, could be connected with that crime beyond any shadow of a doubt. Eyewitness testimony placed him at the scene of Tippit's murder. Moreover, when Oswald was taken into custody, he had a revolver in his possession. Laboratory tests showed that the cartridge casings found near Tippit's body belonged to Oswald's revolver to the exclusion of all other revolvers in the world.

From Tippit's murder, the commission report claimed, it was only a few easy steps to the Kennedy assassination. Investigation of the revolver that killed Tippit revealed that it had been bought from the mail-order division of George Rose & Company, Los Angeles, and had been purchased by someone using the name A. J.

Hidell. Further investigation showed that the rifle found on the sixth floor of the Texas School Book Depository had been purchased from Klein's Sporting Goods, by an A. Hidell.

Three pieces of evidence connected Lee Harvey Oswald with the purchase of the rifle and the revolver. First, when he was captured, Oswald was carrying an identification card with the name Hidell on it. Next, handwriting experts agreed that the handwriting of A. J. Hidell—the man who wrote to George Rose & Company for the revolver—was the same as Oswald's. Finally, the police had found two photographs among Oswald's belongings; both showed Oswald holding the rifle and wearing the revolver in a holster on his hip. Marina Oswald testified that she had taken the pictures the March before the assassination.

This evidence proved, the commission argued, that Oswald owned the rifle that was found on the sixth floor of the Depository. And it could likewise be proved that this was the weapon that had killed Kennedy and wounded Governor Connally. Ballistics tests showed that the bullet casings found in the room on the sixth floor of the Depository belonged to Oswald's rifle. Additional tests showed that the bullet fragments found in the limousine and a nearly whole bullet found on a stretcher at Parkland Memorial Hospital came from that rifle to the exclusion of all other rifles in the world.

There could be no doubt—according to the evidence offered by the Warren Report—that Oswald's rifle, a Mannlicher-Carcano, killed President Kennedy. The commission realized, however, that even if Oswald's rifle had definitely been used in the crime, that was not proof that Oswald had fired the shots. Someone else may have used his rifle in order to throw the blame on Oswald. To convict Oswald of the crime, it would be necessary to show that he had been on the sixth floor of the Depository at the time of the assassination and that he had had the weapon in his possession.

Here again, the commission believed that it had the necessary evidence. Oswald met the description of the assassin given by Howard Brennan, the man who had been standing in the plaza below. In addition, several Depository employees could place Oswald alone on the sixth floor where they had left him to go to lunch one half hour before the shooting took place. Oswald's statement that he was eating lunch with someone named "Junior" at the time of the assassination could simply not have been true. The only "Junior" employed in the Depository was on the fifth floor at the time of the shooting and denied having eaten with Oswald.

There was also other evidence that placed Oswald on the sixth floor and in possession of the rifle. The Dallas police found Oswald's palm print on the Mannlicher-Carcano. No other identifiable prints—Oswald's or those belonging to anyone else—were found on the weapon. Moreover, a paper bag with Oswald's palm print and fingerprints was found on the sixth floor—a paper bag which Oswald may have used to carry the rifle to work in that morning. And a clipboard—the one used by Oswald in his daily chores at the Depository—was found at a spot not far from where the rifle had been discovered.

The commission concluded that Oswald had fired three shots at the President from the sixth floor of the Depository. The first shot may have missed Kennedy entirely and struck the street near the railway overpass, where it splintered off chips of the asphalt pavement. One of the pieces of pavement wounded a bystander, James Tague. The second shot entered the President's back, just below his neck, and then exited from the front

ABOVE: OSWALD'S APPARENT POSITION FOR
THE SHOOTING. THE SCENE IS THE SIXTH FLOOR
OF THE TEXAS SCHOOL BOOK DEPOSITORY.
RIGHT: A VIEW OF THE STREET FROM THE
BOOK DEPOSITORY WINDOW.

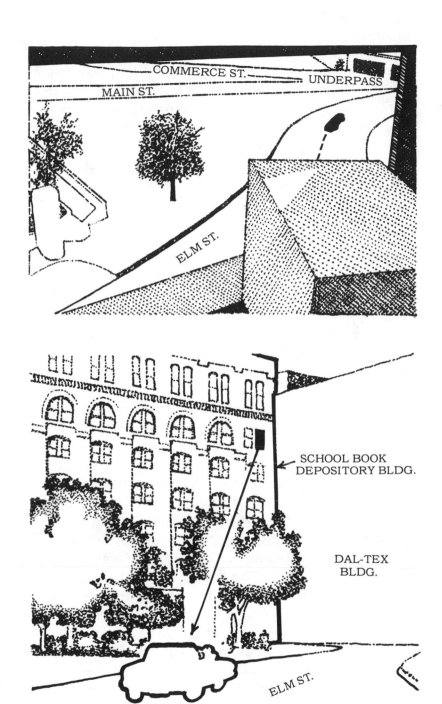

COMMERCE ST.

UNDERPASS

MAIN ST.

ELM ST.

SCHOOL BOOK
DEPOSITORY BLDG.

DAL-TEX
BLDG.

ELM ST.

of his neck. It was this bullet, the report said, that had gone on to wound Governor Connally and was responsible for his collapsed lung, broken rib, and shattered wrist. The third bullet struck Kennedy at the back of the head and caused a wound so severe that recovery would have been impossible.

The commission likewise determined that the three shots were not difficult ones to make and that Oswald had the ability to have fired them. Using a home movie that had been made of the assassination by one of the eyewitnesses, Abraham Zapruder, it was possible to prove that the limousine had been moving at 11 miles (17.5 km) per hour at the time Oswald fired from the Depository. During the time all three shots were fired, the President's body was at a distance of between 177 to 266 feet (53 to 81 m) from the sixth-floor window. Using the telescopic sights on the rifle, that distance was shortened to between 45 and 67 feet (13 to 20 m).

The Zapruder film likewise showed that the two shots which struck Kennedy had been fired within a period of 4.8 to 5.6 seconds. This meant that Oswald had to have been able to shoot twice, in less than 6 seconds, at a slow-moving target which appeared to be less than 70 feet (21 m) from him. Oswald, the commission discovered, had been trained in rifle marksmanship while he was in the Marine Corps. He had failed to win the highest awards offered by the corps in marksmanship, but he had, nevertheless, passed his tests and was judged to be an average shot. The report concluded, therefore, that the shots were within his capabilities—especially if one assumed he was in a highly excited state of mind, with his body and senses geared for the assassination.

The case was now almost complete. The evidence seemed overwhelming. Oswald had owned the rifle responsible for the death of President Kennedy. He had been on the sixth floor of the Depository when the shots were fired. Only one major factor remained for the commission to determine: motive. If Oswald killed Kennedy, why had he killed him? Were his reasons personal, political, or were they linked in some way with the wishes of others?

To discover a motive, the commission staff delved deep into Oswald's past, from the time he was born in New Orleans in 1939 until his death in Dallas. The biography they constructed revealed a life with an unusual degree of unhappiness, frustration, and bitterness. Oswald had been born two months after the death of his father. He had grown up under the care of his mother, Marguerite, a strong-willed, domineering woman who frequently irritated those around her. Mrs. Oswald's two eldest sons had had little to do with their mother once they reached adulthood. Lee Harvey Oswald was the third and youngest son, the baby of the family, and the son closest to his mother.

As a child, Lee had been quiet, withdrawn, and reticent—characteristics he also displayed as an adult. A psychiatrist who examined him when he was thirteen— after Oswald had been picked up for truancy—had found no evidence of insanity. Lee was only lonely and badly in need of friends and encouragement.

At fifteen, Oswald began to read the works of Karl Marx. In spite of a severe reading disability called dyslexia, he read through this difficult, erudite material and was impressed by it. He began to spend a great deal of time in libraries surveying other Communist publications and to call himself a Marxist-Leninist. Because of his dyslexia, Oswald had to work hard to read the books that had come to interest him. When he tried to write his own ideas down, his English was awkward and full of misspellings and grammatical errors.

At seventeen, Oswald enlisted in the Marine Corps. He served for nearly three years. His buddies in the corps remembered him as quiet, but fond of arguing over politics. They recalled on one occasion that he attacked President Eisenhower as unworthy of respect, but defended Nikita Khrushchev, the Premier of the Soviet Union. For Oswald, Khrushchev had become a personal hero. Later, he was to develop a similar respect for Fidel Castro, the leader of the Cuban Revolution and foremost Communist of the Western hemisphere.

Three months before his tour of duty in the Marine Corps was over, Oswald obtained a dependency discharge, claiming that his mother had been the victim of an accident and needed his assistance. He spent only three days at home, however, before he left for New Orleans, where he boarded a ship bound for Britain. Three weeks later he was in Moscow. Full of anger and resentment at what he called the evils of capitalism, he renounced his American citizenship and offered to turn over to the Soviet government secret radar information he had learned when stationed in Atsugi, Japan, a major headquarters for CIA activities in Asia. What he desired, he told Russian authorities, was a chance to reside in a country where he could live by his Communist beliefs openly.

The Russians agreed to let him remain, but turned down his offer of help. They distrusted him and suspected that he might be an enemy agent sent to the Soviet Union to spy. Frustrated and angry, Oswald attempted to commit suicide in his Moscow hotel. The act, however, failed to impress the authorities, who sent him off to Minsk, a city in the western part of the Soviet Union, where he could be watched closely and where he could do little harm. There he was given an apartment, a small income, and a job in a factory that manufactured electronic components for radios and televisions.

At Minsk, Oswald met Marina Prusakova, a young and attractive pharmacist who was the niece of an important Soviet official. Oswald asked Marina to marry him after less than a month of courtship and she agreed. The two set up house in Minsk, but Oswald soon became intensely dissatisfied with life in Russia. He decided that he wanted to return to the United States and bring Marina with him. He petitioned the Soviet government to leave, and wrote to Governor John Connally (whom he thought was still Secretary of the Navy) of Texas, unsuccessfully, asking that his discharge from the Marine Corps, which had been declared dishonorable because of his defection to the Soviet Union, be reviewed and changed to honorable.

In 1962, the American embassy in Moscow loaned Oswald the money he needed to return to the United States. He and Marina arrived soon afterward in Texas. But life in the United States proved difficult and frustrating for him. He found it hard to hold on to a job, and he had his family to take care of. He and Marina began to fight constantly. He did not want her to learn English or to have friends of her own; this way she would remain completely dependent on him. Often their fights would turn violent, and he would beat his wife viciously.

In the last months of his life, Oswald seemed overwhelmed by a sense of failure. On April 5, 1963, he lost the one job he had enjoyed, working in a typography studio. On April 10, he did not return home until very late in the evening. Nervous and excited, he confessed to his wife that he had earlier that day shot Major General Edwin A. Walker, a hero of the extreme right and an opponent of integration. The next day, however, the Oswalds learned that Walker was not dead and had not even been wounded. Lee had failed in his first attempt at assassination.

Sometime later, Oswald boasted to Marina that he was planning another murder. This time, he said, his victim would be the "Vice-President." His wife was not certain whether he meant Lyndon Johnson, who then held that office, or Richard Nixon, the former Vice-President under President Eisenhower. In any case, she grew frightened and locked her husband in the bathroom until he promised to abandon the idea.

In mid-1963, Oswald made two trips that showed the state of mind he was in. The first was to New Orleans, the city of his birth, and the second was to Mexico City. In New Orleans, he held down a menial job that paid little, but wrote Marina that he was doing well. He spent most of his time involved in leftist political work. He founded a "Fair Play for Cuba" committee and seems to have been the only member. He handed out pro-Communist Cuba pamphlets and defended Castro on talk shows. It seemed as though he were attempting to add meaning to his life by a new commitment to Marxism and political activity.

Then in September 1963, only two months before the assassination, Oswald left for Mexico City by bus. On his arrival he went to the Cuban embassy to obtain a visa to travel to Havana, once again to try life in a Communist country. The Cubans, however, turned him down. Oswald met a similar rejection at the Soviet embassy, where he was told a visa would take at least four months to obtain and even then he might not receive one. Oswald had no choice but to return to Dallas and his family.

In this brief outline of Oswald's life, the Warren Report found a motive for the assassination. No single, overriding reason caused him to kill the President. It was a combination of reasons, arising from confusion, anxiety, and discontent with life. The report concluded that Oswald was a man with a great deal of hostility—hostility toward other people in general, toward people in positions of authority, and toward society.

Oswald had often verbally expressed his hatred of the United States, but he had also acted on this hatred. He had abandoned his native country and sought citizenship in the Soviet Union. Yet life in Russia had also disappointed him. He had searched long and hard for the "perfect society," where he could live in peace and contentment, but his search was doomed from the start. It was doomed because he was a man who could be at home nowhere.

But perhaps most importantly, the Warren Report described Oswald as a man with no "meaningful relationships" to help stabilize his life. He had no close friends and his wife was estranged from him. His mother offered no comfort or encouragement. His work provided no sense of security or individual worth; indeed, it barely gave him enough money to support his family. He was, in short, a person who was "perpetually disoriented with the world around him."

In order to overcome his deep sense of failure and disorientation, Oswald looked for an act that would give meaning and importance to his life. First, he attempted to take the life of General Walker and, when that failed, decided to assassinate the Vice-President. Marina prevented that. But finally he succeeded, when he shot and killed President Kennedy. These were the acts, the Warren Report said, of a defeated, frustrated man, who wanted to do something that would make his name known throughout the world. The reticent, retiring Oswald, so easily ignored by those around him, had killed the President in order to prove the seriousness of his political convictions and to get himself into the pages of history. Had Oswald found a worthwhile job, had he obtained a visa to Cuba, had he been able to solve his problems with his wife, he may never have felt the pressing need to commit the act that made him famous. But "Out of these and many other factors," the report concluded, "which may have molded the character of Lee Harvey Oswald, there emerged a man capable of assassinating President Kennedy."

With this description of Oswald's personality, the commission believed it had completed the task set before it. It had proved that Oswald owned the rifle that killed the President and that he had had the opportunity and ability to fire it. And it had supplied the motive which led him to the assassination. During the investigation, the staff had taken testimony from more than five hundred people. Thousands more had been interviewed or had submitted affidavits. Careful consideration had been given to the material evidence in the case, evidence which was substantial and varied. For the commission and for the public at large, it seemed as though everything that could be said about the assassination had been said.

Or so, at least, it seemed for a while. When the report was submitted in September 1964, few people suspected that in less than two years it would find itself strongly challenged and attacked, an object of ridicule and disbelief. At best, the commission would see itself described as inept or badly mistaken in its conclusions. At worst, it would hear itself denounced as having been formed to cover up and distort the truth. In the next three chapters we shall look at what happened to cause this amazing change in public opinion and at what people now believe to be the truth about the assassination.

Chapter Three

THE CRITICS

From the beginning there was a group of individuals who took an active interest in the assassination and its investigation. The press dubbed these people "assassination buffs" or "assassinologists," but they have come to be more familiarly known as just "the critics." What set these people apart from others who took an interest in the case was the depth and intensity of their concern, and a willingness to devote a great deal of time to study and research. The critics avidly collected information from newspapers and magazines. They studied every detail of the Warren Report and pored over the twenty-six volumes of supporting material. What they found disturbed them profoundly. The report, they concluded, was filled with error and mistaken conclusions; it was carelessly put together and settled nothing about the crime it claimed to solve.

The critics came from a variety of backgrounds. Some were reporters and journalists. Others were lawyers, housewives, and college professors. None were professional investigators or criminologists and none had training in scientific evaluation of evidence. What spurred them on in their often difficult and tedious work was an innate curiosity and a conviction that there was a great deal more to be known about the assassination. For the most part, too, they were admirers of the late

President and wanted to be certain that his true assassin had been brought to justice.

The first important critic to gain a nationwide reputation was a New York lawyer named Mark Lane. Lane published his *Rush to Judgment* in 1966. The book soon became a bestseller and its author a popular guest on television talk shows and lecturer before college audiences. More than anyone else, Lane epitomized the critics and their work. Hardworking and deeply committed, he devoted a great deal of his own time and money toward uncovering what he believed to be the truth about Kennedy's murder.

After Lane's *Rush to Judgment,* there came a torrent of books. Edward Jay Epstein's *Inquest* and Sylvia Meagher's *Accessories After the Fact* were the best of the lot, but there were also works by Richard Popkin, Harold Weisberg, Josiah Thompson, and many others.*
One critic, Bernard Fensterwald, a Washington lawyer, helped organize and coordinate an attack on the Warren Commission. Intelligent and experienced in government, he was eventually responsible for the establishment of the Committee to Investigate Assassinations, a private, Washington-based group that collects and analyzes information concerning modern-day assassinations in the United States.

The critics tore into the Warren Report point by point and continued the attack until confidence in the work of the commission was completely undermined. Some of the points they made were insignificant or ultimately discarded as mistakes or errors in judgment. Others, however, were of major importance. To this day, many remain as questions that must be answered if the

* For a more complete listing of the critics and their works, see the "Suggested Readings" at the end of this book.

whole truth about the death of President Kennedy is ever to be known.

One of the earliest and most devastating attacks made by the critics was on the nature of the commission itself. No one doubted the prestige and reputation of its seven most prominent members. They were known to be intelligent, active, and responsible men. But *because* they were important men with careers to pursue, they were at the same time *busy* men, men who had "other fish to fry."

Earl Warren, the chairman of the commission, was also the Chief Justice of the Supreme Court. Russell and Cooper were senators, Boggs and Ford congressmen. Dulles and McCloy were also involved in pursuits that took up most of their time. Each commission member, therefore, could devote only a small portion of his time to the investigation. How could such men, the critics asked, do a thorough report? Wouldn't they tend to look for the simplest and quickest solution possible and avoid evidence that was complicated or troublesome?

There was evidence, the critics said, to suggest that the commission had done just that. From the beginning, the commissioners had set a deadline for their report. They wanted their work completed and their findings submitted to President Johnson before the presidential elections coming up in November. That gave them much less than a year to set up their staff, decide how the investigation should proceed, carry out the investigation, and publish the report. How could a major inquiry, with so much to consider, complete its work in so short a time? Unless, that is, its members had already decided beforehand that they would follow the information only so far and then abandon it when it proved too time-consuming.

Mark Lane termed this a "rush to judgment" and made it the title to his first book on the assassination. Another critic, Edward Jay Epstein, pictured it as a substitution of real facts with what he called "political truth." Political truth looked for an explanation that would lay speculation to rest, Epstein said. It sought to contribute to the stability of the country by offering the solution least frightening to the general public. Any information that might point to a conspiracy was ignored or passed over. At the same time, any evidence showing that Oswald had committed the crime alone was accepted and emphasized. The result, Epstein said, was a one-sided and biased report that turned its back on important information and clues.

Another point that bothered the critics about the commission was its failure to set up its own investigative unit. To be sure, the commission had its staff, but this staff relied heavily on evidence and data collected by the FBI and the CIA. This meant that the commission was much less independent and self-sufficient than it should have been. It meant that the staff and commissioners formed their opinions based not on their own research, but on the research already done for them by the FBI and the CIA.

There were two problems with this method of operation, the critics said. First, it tended to turn the commission into a mouthpiece for the two federal agencies and their investigations into the assassination. But more importantly, there was no way for the commission to tell whether the information it received was accurate and complete. Indeed, the critics were able to prove that, on at least one occasion, the FBI destroyed information—a letter from Oswald to an FBI agent in Dallas mailed only a few days before Kennedy's death—that might have proved important. And they were likewise able to show that both the FBI and CIA withheld pertinent data from the commission when the agencies considered that data "top secret" or feared that it might reveal too much about the secret inner workings of their organizations. Moreover, the critics learned that the commissioners had frequently hesitated to challenge J. Edgar Hoover, the powerful head of the FBI, when they wanted to know something more about some facet of the case. How could an adequate inquiry be held, they asked, if the commission was afraid to ask questions? How could it be certain of its conclusions, if the evidence it had been given was incomplete and even doctored?

The critics had grave questions, too, about the evidence submitted by the Warren Report as "proof" that Oswald had killed Kennedy. They had strong doubts, for instance, that the rifle found on the sixth floor of the Book Depository, the Mannlicher-Carcano, could have fired the shots it was supposed to have fired.

Italians who had used that make of weapon in World War II knew it to be inaccurate and of poor quality. Further, the FBI found that the rifle Oswald possessed was in very bad condition, worn and rusted. A marksman chosen to test the rifle refused to do so; he believed the firing pin might easily break. Finally, the telescopic sights on the rifle could not be properly aligned with a target and were designed for a left-handed person, while Oswald had been right-handed. How could such a rifle have been used to kill the President?

Moreover, the critics reasoned, the shots that killed Kennedy and wounded Connally had not been easy shots. When he was a marine, Oswald had scored relatively low in marksmanship. The shots that day in

Dallas involved three firings within 7.1 seconds at a moving target, a target that was at times hidden by the leaves and branches of an oak tree.

The commission set up an experiment to see if it could duplicate Oswald's achievement. It hired three *expert* riflemen and allowed them to shoot at a *stationary* target, using telescopic sights that were in *good* condition—and yet the three experts failed to score bull's-eyes within the time allotted them. How could Oswald, using a rifle that was old and rusty, make the shots the experts could not make? Could the commission really believe that he had shown a marksmanship ability in this one instance that he had never been able to demonstrate under the ideal conditions of a marine practice range?

The critics also believed that the commission had failed to account for all the evidence concerning the bullets and wounds involved in the assassination. What particularly bothered them was the second bullet. This bullet, the report said, struck Kennedy in the back, exited from his throat, and then went on to wound Governor Connally in the chest, causing his lung to collapse and shattering his wrist before it came to rest in his thigh. It was necessary for the second bullet to have done all this, the commission said, since the first and third shots could easily be accounted for: the first had struck the road ahead of the limousine and the third had fatally wounded the President. Furthermore, Oswald did not have time to get off a fourth shot, because his rifle did not fire rapidly enough.

The critics sarcastically called this explanation the "magic-bullet" theory. For them, it was inconceivable that a bullet that had severely wounded two men, tearing bone and tissue as it went through their bodies, could have emerged almost intact from the governor's

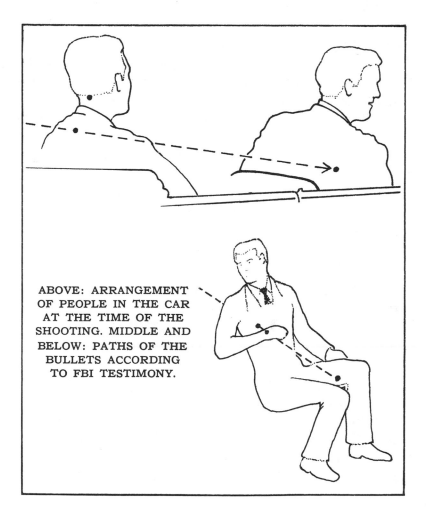

ABOVE: ARRANGEMENT OF PEOPLE IN THE CAR AT THE TIME OF THE SHOOTING. MIDDLE AND BELOW: PATHS OF THE BULLETS ACCORDING TO FBI TESTIMONY.

thigh. Yet this was what the commission asked the public to accept, since the bullet in question was almost complete and undamaged. It had been found that way on one of the stretchers used to carry the wounded men to Parkland Memorial Hospital.

The commission conducted tests to see if a bullet fired into the wrist of a cadaver would emerge intact. It didn't. The bullet came out twisted and flattened. How had a similar bullet, which had done much more damage to Kennedy and Connally, remained almost perfectly formed, losing only a small portion of its weight? For the critics, this was proof that the "magic-bullet" theory had to be revised and a new explanation found which better fit the available evidence. And the one conclusion that seemed to fit this evidence was that Oswald had had an accomplice: there had been a second assassin who had fired the additional bullet. Governor Connally, too, has expressed dissatisfaction with the "magic-bullet" explanation.

There was also other evidence indicating that Connally had been wounded by a separate bullet. When the film taken by Abraham Zapruder was examined closely, two unusual details were noticed. First, there was an interval between the time that President Kennedy was wounded in the back and the time Governor Connally reacted to his wounds. If both men had been wounded by the same shot, how could this interval be accounted for?

The Warren Report speculated that the gap was due to a "delayed reaction" on the part of Governor Connally, and pointed out that many people wounded by a rifle bullet are not at first aware that they have been shot. The governor had been wounded, but he did not feel the pain and discomfort until later. For the critics, however, the gap was too long to be explained by a "delayed reaction" and was proof that another solution had to be devised.

The second controversial aspect of the Zapruder film concerned the head wound that killed the President. In the film, Kennedy can be seen reacting to the shot by first moving slightly forward and then hurtling suddenly and forcefully backward—as though the bullet that hit his head had come from the *front,* and not from *behind.* Since Oswald had been in the Book Depository, behind the President, he could not have fired the fatal shot. That shot, the critics argued, must have come from the grassy knoll or from the railway overpass.

Indeed, there was eyewitness testimony that confirmed this supposition. Many who had been at Dealey Plaza that day believed that the shots had come from the knoll. One witness described the "suspicious behavior" she had seen on the knoll—a movement of cars and men that suggested preparation for an assassination and a subsequent getaway. Another had seen smoke on the knoll after the shots were fired—smoke that could have come from a rifle. Yet the Warren Commission had ignored this testimony and had chosen to believe only those witnesses who said the shots came from the Depository. On what basis, the critics asked, did the commission accept one kind of testimony, yet refuse to accept another? How could the report be certain that shots had not come from the knoll?

As they looked over the work of the commission, the critics found yet another reason for dissatisfaction. They discovered that the official autopsy, performed at the National Naval Medical Center in Bethesda, Maryland, when the President's body was returned to Washington, had been mishandled and incompetently done. Not one of the doctors assigned to this important task had had wide experience doing autopsies, an unusual oversight, since there was no lack of experts available. Indeed, Dr. Cyril Wecht, a past president of the American Academy of Forensic Sciences, would later call the autopsy performed, "worse than no autopsy at all."

The most glaring error the Bethesda crew committed was a failure to probe the wound they found in the President's back, just below his neck. Instead of examining it fully, as a more experienced group would have done, the doctors studied it only to a finger's depth. Had the bullet exited from the President's neck? The doctors failed to answer this important question. A proper examination of the wound could have determined the bullet's course through Kennedy's body and thereby vindicated the commission's conclusion that the bullet had gone on to wound Governor Connally. But since no examination had been made, no one could say if the bullet had remained in the President's body or if it had exited from the neck. Yet the commission claimed with certainty that the bullet had left the President's body.

To make matters even worse, it was discovered that the doctors who attempted to save Kennedy's life at Parkland Memorial Hospital in Dallas had come to a conclusion that was very different from the conclusion of the Bethesda doctors. The Parkland doctors judged the wound in the front of the President's neck to be an *entrance* wound, because it was clean and neat. An exit wound, they believed, would have shown signs of torn flesh, flesh that had been disturbed as the bullet left the body. The doctors at the Naval Medical Center said that the neck wound was an *exit* wound. Who, then, was right? The question could only have been answered by a thorough and complete autopsy, but none had been done. The problem was more than academic. An entrance wound in the front of the neck would mean that the President had been shot from the front, by someone other than Oswald.

There were other discrepancies between the findings of the two sets of doctors that bothered the critics. First, testimony varied as to the location of the wound in the back. The FBI, which had access to both autopsies, said the wound was in one spot. The Bethesda autopsy, however, described the wound as 4 inches (10 cm) lower. This seemed too great a distance to be the result of a casual mistake. But where exactly was the wound? If it were in the spot claimed by the FBI, then the bullet might well have exited from his neck. But if it were in the spot located by the Bethesda crew, the bullet may well have entered the President's body too low to exit from his neck and therefore could not have gone on to wound Governor Connally.

Second, there was the matter of the tracheotomy—the incision made in Kennedy's neck by the Parkland doctors to help him breathe more easily. The doctors had made a small incision on the spot where he had been wounded. By the time the President's body arrived at Bethesda, however, the cut had become greatly enlarged. What had happened to turn a small, surgical incision into a large cut with irregular edges? The critics suggested a grisly possibility: the tracheotomy had been purposely enlarged, perhaps when the President's body was in transit from Dallas, to make it impossible for anyone to tell whether the original neck wound had been an exit or an entrance wound.

Finally, the critics were dissatisfied with the motive the Warren Report ascribed to Oswald. The commission said that Oswald had killed Kennedy in order to make a name for himself and enter the pages of history. But if this were so, why did Oswald deny any connection with the assassination after he was captured? If he had wanted to become famous, wouldn't he have confessed, even boasted, about his crime? Instead, he claimed that given time he would prove himself not guilty.

The commission said that Oswald was a disturbed individual, a man with few friends, and with an "overriding hostility to his environment." His discontentment and anger had grown so severe that he had become capable of any act, including assassination, that he felt might relieve his anxiety. But if this were so, the critics asked, why did so many people testify—people who had known Oswald well—that he was neither violent nor aggressive? The police who questioned Oswald after the assassination found him sane and rational. Even J. Edgar Hoover, the head of the FBI, wrote that there was "no indication at all that Oswald was a man addicted to violence."

Indeed, one critic, Edward Jay Epstein, believed that much of the portrait of Oswald painted by the Warren Report was badly mistaken and wrongheaded. In his book *Legend: The Secret World of Lee Harvey Oswald*, Epstein argued that Oswald was not the pathetic, bungling, and half-educated man the commission made him out to be. On many occasions, Oswald had impressed people who met him with his erudition and intelligence —people who came to the conclusion that he was "at least" a college graduate. The Oswald described in the report, Epstein concluded, was a "myth" concocted by men who needed a disturbed individual in order to find a motive for the assassination. If Oswald was not "disturbed," then the motive ascribed to him would fall apart.

If there was little or no evidence to prove that Oswald sought fame or was prone to violence or was "disturbed," what had been his motive for committing the assassination? This question could not be answered satisfactorily, the critics said, until a great deal more information about Oswald's past was uncovered. The Warren Commission, they argued, had indeed "rushed to judgment."

It had assumed from the beginning that Oswald, and only Oswald, was guilty, and then had derived a motive to fit the crime. A more complete investigation would look at all the evidence, with no prior prejudice against Oswald.

Eventually, the combined efforts of the critics helped to destroy the credibility of the Warren Report and the commission which had produced it. The critics found their attacks and charges readily accepted by a public anxious to buy and read the books the critics produced. In 1966—the year that saw the publication of the first two major critical attacks—a Gallup poll showed that 66 percent of the American people no longer believed the report. By 1975, four out of five Americans no longer found it convincing.

The general public was not alone. Governor John Connally, the man severely wounded that day in Dallas, was certain that the report was inaccurate on several important points. Lyndon Johnson, the President responsible for the appointment of the commission, also believed the whole truth had not been uncovered. Even two men who served on the commission—Senator Richard Russell and Congressman Hale Boggs—eventually announced their dissatisfaction with the report and acknowledged that they now had serious doubts about its conclusions.

Had the commission followed every lead suggested by the evidence or had it followed only the leads that pointed to Oswald? Why had the official autopsy been so badly botched? How could Oswald, using a rifle that was second-rate and himself no marksman, make shots that stumped the experts? Could a single bullet really have wounded both Kennedy and Connally and yet remain in almost perfect condition?

These questions and others bothered the public as they bothered the critics. Few people now believed that the commission had settled the problem of the assassination. But if the commission had been wrong, what was the truth? What explanation best fit the facts in the case and took into consideration the discoveries made by the critics?

The answer was simple: conspiracy. The President had been killed by a group of people of whom Oswald was only one. Conspiracy was the one solution that seemed to pull together all the loose ends. If there had been more than one assassin at Dealey Plaza, the critics argued, that would explain why some witnesses heard shots coming from the grassy knoll, while others heard them coming from the Depository. If there had been two or more assassins, the mystery surrounding the President's wounds could be accounted for—one assassin had shot at him from the front, a second from behind.

But most importantly, the critics pointed out, conspiracy gave Lee Harvey Oswald a motive for the crime and helped explain how a man so often described as a misfit and a loser could have planned and carried out the murder of a President of the United States. Oswald had had the assistance of others; they had trained him, given him the necessary support, and convinced him that the President should be shot.

But if Oswald did not act alone, who had helped him? On this question, the critics rarely agreed. Instead, they developed a variety of opinions which have been widely discussed and debated to this day. None of the theories, however, has emerged as the leading contender and definitive explanation for the assassination. In the next chapter, we shall take a look at some of these theories and the reasons their defenders give for accepting them.

Chapter Four

CONSPIRACY?

There have been many theories about the assassination of President Kennedy. Most of them have been unconvincing or outlandish, or have departed from the evidence too drastically to be accepted as possible solutions to the crime. Others have simply lacked the ring of truth and probability. Few people, for instance, could believe in plots hatched by the Dallas police, by a trusted Kennedy aide, or by Mrs. Lyndon Johnson, the wife of the Vice-President. Yet these were all explanations offered as indisputable in the early years after the assassination.

There have been five theories, however, that have stood the test of time and proved persuasive to large numbers of people. These five have frequently been discussed and debated and have been the subject of numerous books, magazine articles, and television documentaries. Each of them has its own strong arguments and its own way of looking at the facts. Each theory has identified a group with a credible motive—a wish to see the President dead—and with the means and ability to carry out its intention. Without these two factors—motive and capability—no conspiracy theory would be worthy of consideration.

* The conspiracy theory that has had the widest appeal has been the belief that President Kennedy was the victim of an international Communist plot. Those who defend this theory claim that they have a lot of evidence to support their conclusion. After all, they point out, the accused assassin, Lee Harvey Oswald, had been an avowed Communist. From the time he was fifteen, Oswald had read Marx and had called himself a Marxist-Leninist. To anyone willing to listen, he spoke of his preference for the Communist economic system and Communist politics and his disgust with capitalism. In 1959, he acted on his beliefs by going to Russia, where he denounced his American citizenship and declared his wish to become a citizen of the Soviet Union.

For many Americans, such an attitude was not only strange and unusual, it was also criminal and traitorous. The Communists were sworn enemies of the United States. On many occasions, they had boasted that they would destroy America and its way of life. Whether this boast was serious or merely a part of Cold War rhetoric, perhaps no one could say with any certainty. But millions of Americans did not doubt that the Soviet Union was already secretly at work in the United States to make good its threat. Was Oswald part of these secret plans? Had he received training in Russia to act as an assassin and then been sent back to the United States to help undermine and destroy American society?

These questions were made more urgent by the fact that Cuba, only 90 miles (144 km) from the American mainland, had recently become a Communist nation. Castro, the Cuban leader, was known to hate the United States and to distrust President Kennedy. During his first year in office, Kennedy had sponsored an invasion of Cuba to force Castro out of office. The Bay of Pigs invasion, as it was known, had failed, but it had angered the Cuban leader and made him fear that Kennedy might attempt a similar invasion at another time. In addition, Castro knew that the CIA had planned several attempts against his life, plots he may well have believed came from the orders of President Kennedy.

Castro seemed to have had ample reason to want President Kennedy dead. He may have contacted Oswald and made arrangements for the assassination, plans which Oswald then proceeded to carry out. The defenders of this theory argue that the Communists accomplished two things by the murder of the President. First, they eliminated a threat to Castro's life and to Cuba. But more importantly, they hoped Kennedy's death would cause a severe disturbance in American life, which might lead to widespread dissatisfaction and an ultimate weakening of the United States.

* A second conspiracy theory completely reversed the conclusions of the first. Promoters of this explanation are convinced that Kennedy had been killed by anti-Castro Cubans who had come to hate the President because of his failure to destroy the Castro regime. The anti-Castroites reasoned that, with Kennedy off the scene, a new President who would be more sympathetic to their cause might come into office and order a new and more successful invasion of Cuba.

There were several anti-Castro organizations in the United States dedicated to violence and terrorism. Located in the Miami area and in other places where there were large numbers of Cubans who had fled Castro's Communist regime, these groups collected weapons and ammunition and trained their members in preparation for a return to Cuba. They hated Castro passionately; in many instances he had been responsible for confiscating their property in Cuba or for imprisoning or putting to death relatives and friends. The Cuban exiles also hated anyone who supported Castro in any way.

The Cubans in America grew to dislike Kennedy soon after he became President. They blamed him for the failure of the Bay of Pigs invasion, and they feared that he had begun working toward establishing normal relations with Castro's Cuba. The exiles knew that they would never be able to return to their homeland if the United States and Cuba were to settle their differences. To keep their cause alive, they decided that the President would have to be eliminated and began to search for an assassin. Eventually, they settled on Oswald.

The major difficulty for those who support this theory is Oswald's Communist background, a background that would seemingly keep him distant from the anti-Castro Cubans. But a connection could be made. When he had been in New Orleans a few months before the assassination, Oswald had been friendly not only with Castro sympathizers, but also with Cuban exiles closely associated with anti-Castro activities. He had offered them his services as an ex-marine, to help train guerrillas that could go to Cuba to fight Castro. He even suggested terrorist tactics that might be carried out in the United States in order to dramatize the plight of the Cuban exiles and their hatred for Castro.

Moreover, there was the Warren Commission testimony of Mrs. Sylvia Odio that connected Oswald with the anti-Castroites. Mrs. Odio was a leader in the Cuban-exile community in Dallas. About a month before the assassination, Mrs. Odio claimed, she had been visited by three men. Two were expatriate Cubans, she said. The third was a quiet young man whose name she remembered as "Leon Oswald." The three had asked her for money and when she refused, they had left.

The next day, one of the three returned to her home. "What did you think of the American?" he asked. "Our idea is to introduce him to the underground in Cuba, because he is great, he is kind of nuts." Then he went on to say: "Kennedy should have been assassinated after the Bay of Pigs." He chided Mrs. Odio for her lack of courage and commitment and suggested that things would be better for the Cuban exiles if they would not hesitate to use violence when it was needed.

The Warren Commission decided to reject Mrs. Odio's statement because the FBI found three men, including an Oswald look-alike, who said they were the three who had visited her. But to others, her testimony sounded like the truth and raised too many questions. Why, for instance, was she certain that one of the men had been named Leon Oswald? Why had the man she identified as Oswald have so many of the character traits possessed by the real Oswald? Besides, the three men had told her they were on their way from New Orleans to another destination, and the real Oswald had been in New Orleans at that time and could have made the trip to Dallas with two Cubans he had befriended and had offered to help.

The supporters of the anti-Castro conspiracy theory believe that the Cuban exiles had reason to want Kennedy dead and had the ability and means to carry out that desire. The choice of Oswald to be the assassin had been a stroke of genius and good luck. Oswald was an avowed Communist. If he were the assassin, the anti-Castro cause would gain in two ways. First, President Kennedy would be dead, and second, American anger over the assassination would be directed against Communist Cuba. And that anger might lead to another invasion, one that would bring Castro to his knees.

* A third conspiracy theory implicates the Mafia, or organized crime, as it is sometimes called. In many ways, the Mafia was an obvious choice. Over the years, it had learned to be wary of President Kennedy and his younger brother Robert. In the fifties, Robert had served as counsel to the Senate Committee on Rackets, where he investigated union corruption. The investigation uncovered close ties between some union leaders and important figures in organized crime, ties indicating that the Mafia had a powerful influence on several unions and might ultimately destroy the labor movement in the United States. The investigation was also responsible for sending Jimmy Hoffa, the president of the teamster's union, to prison. Robert Kennedy made no secret of the fact that he hoped to put many other corrupt union leaders and members of organized crime behind bars.

When John Kennedy became President of the United States in 1961, he appointed Robert to serve as his Attorney General, the head of the Department of Justice. The two Kennedy brothers decided that one of the principal activities of the new Administration would be to limit the power of organized crime and break its hold on American life. As a result, the federal government began to prepare a systematic attack on the Mafia, an attack President Kennedy hoped to continue into his second Administration and perhaps complete.

But organized crime also had other reasons to dislike President Kennedy. For years, the Mafia had flourished in Cuba, where it owned or had investments in gambling casinos, nightclubs, resort hotels, and so on. The pre-Castro regime tolerated the Mafia and shared in its profits. But when Castro came to power, he put an end to organized crime in Cuba. It is estimated that the

Mafia lost hundreds of millions of dollars in investments and income—a loss that could never be regained as long as Castro remained in power. Like the anti-Castro Cubans, the Mafia hoped Kennedy would crush the Cuban dictator and restore the old government. And like the Cuban exiles, it grew discouraged when he failed. Clearly, Castro would remain in power as long as Kennedy was in office. An invasion of Cuba could be mounted only when another President assumed the office and took a more aggressive attitude toward Communism.

For those who believed in the Mafia-conspiracy theory, the connection between Lee Harvey Oswald and the underworld was easy to establish. This connection was Jack Ruby, the man who killed Oswald in the basement of the Dallas police building. Ruby was intimately involved with the Mafia and had many friends among its members. As a young man, he had run errands for Al Capone, a famous Mafia boss, and eventually had graduated to more sinister activities. Ruby's name was associated with several gangland murders and brutal beatings. It was also believed that Ruby had been sent to Dallas by the Mafia and given financial backing to set up a nightclub that would act as a front for a lucrative Mexican drug-running business.

There was one other curious fact about the assassination that suggested that organized crime might be involved. When the police sealed off the Dal-Tex Building, a large building near Dealey Plaza, moments after the assassination, they arrested Eugene Hale Brading, a man inside the building who seemed to have no genuine reason for being there. Brading, who described himself simply as an oilman, claimed to have come inside to find a telephone and make a call. After two or three hours, the police released him. Only later was it discovered that Brading's close friends included several powerful figures in organized crime. What had Brading been doing in the area at the time of the assassination? Was he somehow connected with the murder?

When all this information was pulled together, it seemed to indicate something. First, organized crime had a motive to kill the President; Kennedy's death could mean an end to the investigation of the Mafia. Second, the Mafia had the means and ability to kill Kennedy. Organized crime often made use of professional killers, trained to eliminate enemies quickly and efficiently. These killers might well have been the true assassins of President Kennedy, while Oswald was a patsy or a stooge set up to take the blame. Eugene Hale Brading had been at Dealey Plaza to help coordinate the assassination. Jack Ruby had appeared on the scene two days later to kill Oswald and thereby destroy any chance Oswald might have had to prove his innocence.

The Mafia-conspiracy theory had the virtue of neatness. Its target was a segment of American society known to be violent and lawless. It explained why Oswald claimed innocence and why Ruby killed him. But *proving* the Mafia's involvement was another thing. The members of organized crime rarely talk about their activities or, if they do, rarely live to testify in court or before an investigative committee. If President Kennedy were indeed the victim of organized crime, we shall probably never know the whole truth concerning his death.

* A fourth conspiracy theory blames the Central Intelligence Agency for the assassination. Those who espouse this theory argue that there is strong reason to believe that Oswald had worked for the CIA. When he was in the marines, Oswald had served part of his time

as a radar specialist in Atsugi, Japan. Atsugi happened to be one of the largest and most important CIA bases in Asia. Its job was to monitor information received from Communist China, North Korea, and the eastern part of the Soviet Union. When investigators examined the military records concerning Oswald's stay at Atsugi, they discovered that they had been altered to disguise his duties at the base. If there had been nothing to conceal, why had the records been changed? If Oswald had been at Atsugi merely as a marine, why should anyone take the trouble to hide that fact?

The critics also point to other curious facts suggesting that Oswald was no "ordinary citizen." When he left the marines, Oswald had gone immediately to the Soviet Union. How had he financed this trip? How had he made the arrangements so quickly and easily? Had he been sent to Russia to spy, with CIA agents helping every step of the way? Had his mission been to gain acceptance in Russia and later begin his real espionage work?

Furthermore, how had Oswald's return to the United States been arranged? Here was a man who had openly denounced his American citizenship and offered his services to an enemy nation. Yet when he returned to the United States, the CIA failed to investigate him or keep track of his activities. Did the CIA fail to check on Oswald due to gross negligence or had it known about him all along, since he was already one of its agents?

After their arrival in Dallas, Oswald and Marina were befriended by George de Mohrenschildt. De Mohrenschildt was a prominent member of a Russian-exile community in Dallas and had done work for the CIA on several occasions. The friendship between the middle-aged de Mohrenschildts, who were of aristocratic origin, and the Oswalds struck the critics who looked into Oswald's past as odd and inexplicable. What did the two couples have in common? Differences in age, background, and education would have seemed impossible to bridge. Unless, of course, de Mohrenschildt acted secretly as Oswald's contact with the CIA and the friendship was just a cover to disguise this fact.

Those who accused the CIA of involvement in the Kennedy assassination had no trouble proving that the agency had the ability and the motive to kill the President. Over the years, the CIA had been implicated in numerous political murders and assassination attempts throughout the world. It had been accused of the deaths of President Diem in South Vietnam, Lumumba in the Congo, Duvalier in Haiti, Trujillo in the Dominican Republic, and of repeated attempts on the life of Cuba's Castro. Such activities, the critics argue, had given the CIA the experience necessary to plan and carry out the assassination of President Kennedy. Was it so hard to believe that an agency which had used murder in the past to eliminate foreign enemies would also feel free to kill an American President who stood in its way?

And there were important CIA officials, the critics claim, who believed that Kennedy was dangerous to their organization and the work it hoped to carry out in the future. These officials had come to dislike the President because they thought him "soft" on Communism. They distrusted his liberal and moderate policies and feared that he did not have the necessary courage to defend American interests in Cuba, in South Vietnam, or in any nation threatened by Communist subversion. These men, the theory continues, decided that Kennedy had to be eliminated simply because his Administration posed too great a threat to the safety of the American people.

There was still another reason that caused the CIA to

fear the President. After the ill-fated Bay of Pigs invasion, Kennedy's relationship with the CIA had deteriorated. Kennedy blamed the failure of the invasion on bad advice the agency had given him. He believed the agency had grown too powerful and began to consider plans for its reorganization. He wanted a CIA responsive to the orders of the President and not one that acted completely on its own with no regard for any outside restraint.

The threat of a presidential investigation and reorganization was deeply troubling to many CIA agents. They feared that such an investigation would expose the secret activities of the agency to public view. The names of secret agents involved in highly sensitive and important operations would become known and their activities would be compromised. Years of difficult and painstaking work would be destroyed. The CIA would find it hard, if not impossible, to perform the duties it was supposed to perform. Forced to choose between eventual reorganization and "business as usual," the CIA opted for the latter course, and this meant that the President would have to be eliminated. With Kennedy dead, the threat to the organization would end.

In the past decade, the CIA-conspiracy theory has grown in popularity. In that time, a great deal of evidence has come to light showing that the agency has frequently violated American laws and misused the power entrusted to it. On many occasions it has operated clandestinely within the United States, an activity specifically denied it by its constitution. If the CIA has been so willing to violate the law and the rights of American citizens, the critics argue, is it so difficult to imagine that it might choose to assassinate a President, particularly when that President was viewed as a serious threat to the agency itself?

* A fifth conspiracy theory blames the assassination on a combination of anti-Castro Cubans, organized crime, and elements in the CIA. As we have seen, there are critics who believe that each of these three groups had its own strong motives for wanting President Kennedy dead. What led to this new theory was the discovery that they not only had interests in common, but also that they had all worked together on several occasions.

The link between the Mafia and the CIA is an old one, and goes back to the time of World War II, when what was to become the CIA was known as the OSS (Office of Strategic Services). Organized crime in the United States at that time had many contacts with the Mafia in Sicily and on the Italian mainland. Since American troops were about to invade Italy, it was decided that an excellent way to prepare the Italians for the invasion was to use the Mafia connection.

The Mafia helped organize towns and districts in Italy to receive the American troops. It helped turn Italian public opinion against the fascist government and against the German troops that had occupied the country. In the United States the Mafia aided the war effort by helping to keep American ports free of people who might commit sabotage. In return for its assistance, the Mafia was given positions of political power in Sicily after the American occupation of the island, while back in the United States, criminal charges against leading Mafia figures were dropped or forgotten.

The relationship continued to grow after the war. The CIA would call upon the Mafia to perform certain activities and the Mafia would receive special rewards for its efforts. In the late fifties, Robert Kennedy uncovered this strange partnership when he worked for the Senate Rackets Committee. On one occasion, he interrogated a witness—a man known to be associated with organized crime—who refused to answer questions because he had been given immunity by the CIA. The man's claim turned out to be true. He had never been officially associated with the agency in any way. But due to his work as a member of the Mafia he had received immunity from questioning and prosecution. If the CIA-Mafia relationship were this close, the critics asked, was there any way to tell where it stopped? How much "dirty work" had organized crime done for the CIA? Did that "dirty work" include a joint effort to kill President Kennedy?

But it was the CIA and Mafia connection with anti-Castro Cubans that completed the conspiracy, according to this theory. Some anti-Castro Cubans did work for the agency, a few as full-time agents, others as part-time, hired when their services were needed. The Cuban exiles and the CIA had planned and carried out several attempts on Castro's life and had cooperated on the ill-fated Bay of Pigs invasion. Evidence of the relationship between the exiles and the CIA was further substantiated in 1972, when former CIA agents and anti-Castro Cubans were among those arrested for illegally entering the Democratic National Committee headquarters in the Watergate in Washington, D.C. These men, who had worked together frequently in the past, had been given their orders by influential Republicans who wanted them to spy on Democratic activities. The Cubans and former agents claimed that their illegal entry was justifiable on personal grounds. They said they feared that the Democratic party was planning to recognize Castro's Communist government, and they wanted to do what they could to prevent this.

The ties among the CIA, the Mafia, and the anti-Castro Cubans form a complete circle, the critics claim, and the implications are too rich to ignore. Oswald was known to have been associated with two of the groups. He had friends in the Cuban-exile community, and he was suspected of having been a CIA agent. Moreover, Jack Ruby, the man who killed Oswald, had been involved with the Mafia. Had Oswald been part of an assassination conspiracy hatched by all three groups? Had he perhaps been chosen as an ideal "patsy"—a man on whom the guilt could be pinned, while the assassins went free? Only a new investigation of the assassination, the critics argue, could determine the facts. The Warren Commission, they say, failed to look into these very real possibilities and stood discredited.

The five hypotheses discussed above are considered the most likely explanations for the assassination by those who had looked at the evidence and could not believe, as the Warren Commission had, that Lee Harvey Oswald had acted alone. Each of these theories has strong arguments and a persuasive way of looking at the facts in the case. Taken alone, each seems that it might indeed have the answers to the questions raised by the critics.

But at the same time the theories share one glaring fault. None of them provides actual names of people who might have acted as accomplices to Oswald nor any solid evidence that could be used to convict anyone other than Oswald for the crime. The five theories amount to little more than speculation, rational and defensible speculation perhaps, but nevertheless speculation. They add to our general knowledge of the case, but do not provide *specific* names and other concrete data that would prove criminal conspiracy beyond the shadow of a doubt. Until the sort of "hard" evidence the American court system demands can be found, each theory will remain in the realm of the possible, but can never be accepted as a final statement of truth.

One of the problems with the speculations surrounding the death of President Kennedy is that they too easily become clouded with emotion and personal bias. Conservative and moderate Americans tend to believe that the assassination had been carried out by Communists; liberals and radicals are certain that it had been the work of the CIA, the Mafia, or the Cuban exiles. Any investigation focused on supporting a political belief is bound to fail. In the next chapter we shall see how the work of an ambitious and unscrupulous district attorney nearly destroyed rational discussion about the assassination and how some critics, blinded by their own desire to know the final explanation for the crime, supported and urged him on.

Chapter Five

THE GARRISON AFFAIR
AND ITS AFTERMATH

In March 1967, "Big Jim" Garrison, the district attorney of Orleans Parish, Louisiana, announced that he knew the true identity of President Kennedy's assassins. Immediately, the attention of people throughout the world was focused in his direction. "My staff and I solved the assassination weeks ago," Garrison said. "I wouldn't say this if we didn't have evidence beyond a shadow of a doubt. We know the key individuals, the cities involved, and how it was done."

The district attorney told reporters that he had begun his investigation only days after Kennedy's death. What spurred him to look into the matter was a tip that a pilot who lived in New Orleans had been hired by the assassins to serve as a getaway man. Garrison did some checking and decided that the most likely suspect was David William Ferrie. Ferrie was a strange man, known to have founded his own religion with its own peculiar rites and to have kept hundreds of white mice in his apartment, where he experimented with them to discover a cure for cancer. But more importantly, Ferrie was a strong anti-Communist and anti-Castroite, a man with friends in organized crime, and may have done jobs on occasion for the CIA.

There were two things about Ferrie that disturbed

Garrison. First, there was a witness who claimed he had seen Ferrie and Lee Harvey Oswald together at an airport near New Orleans. If it could be proved that Oswald and Ferrie had known each other, Garrison thought, it might be easy to prove that they had conspired to assassinate Kennedy.

The second discovery that disturbed Garrison was that Ferrie and some companions had been in Dallas the weekend of the assassination. According to Ferrie, they had made the long trip to celebrate the acquittal of a friend in organized crime who had been on trial for various charges. Ferrie said that he and his friends had planned to go ice-skating and to do some duck hunting. The problem was, Garrison said, the men had taken no guns with them, nor did they actually skate when they arrived at the ice-skating rink. Instead, they just waited there. It was the day after the assassination, and the rink's manager recalled that Ferrie had made one telephone call and after receiving another one, had left with his friends.

Garrison interpreted Ferrie's strange conduct as proof that he was in some way involved with Kennedy's death. Other evidence of the conspiracy, however, came painfully slow. Ferrie denied that he had known Oswald and said that he had not been part of a plot to kill the President. Garrison abandoned the case momentarily and let it drift until late in 1966, only to take it up again with renewed energy and interest.

Garrison now learned about an important meeting that was supposed to have taken place in New Orleans in 1962. David William Ferrie was at this meeting, along with W. Guy Bannister, a former FBI agent and a man active in right-wing causes, Carlos Quiroda, a Cuban exile, and someone named "Leon Oswald." Without pausing to carefully check the reliability of this information, Garrison accepted it as proof that he was moving in the right direction.

Word then came to the district attorney's office from a man in Baton Rouge, who claimed to have known Ferrie well and to have information pertinent to the investigation. Garrison had the man, whose name was Perry Raymond Russo, questioned, and learned from him that on several occasions Ferrie had spoken of how easy it would be to kill the President and then escape to a foreign country. Russo, however, made no mention of a specific plot and could not say whether Ferrie had been involved in the assassination.

It was not until Garrison had Russo questioned again, under the influence of "truth serum," and later while under hypnosis, that new details began to appear in his testimony. Now Russo remembered a party at Ferrie's apartment in September 1963, only two months before the assassination. At the party, three men had discussed their plans to murder the President and Russo claimed that he had overheard their conversation. The three men had been Ferrie, someone named "Leon Oswald," and a tall, white-haired man named "Clay Bertrand."

Ferrie and Oswald were easily identifiable, but who was Clay Bertrand? Garrison recalled that that name had popped up before in the case, nearly three years earlier. Dean Adams Andrews, a New Orleans lawyer, had told the Secret Service that he had been contacted the day after the assassination by a man who asked him to go to Dallas and defend Lee Harvey Oswald. That man, Andrews said, had identified himself as Clay Bertrand. Andrews told the Warren Commission that Bertrand was a "boy" about 5 feet 6 inches (1.65 m) tall. Later he told the FBI that the whole story was a hoax and that he had never received the call from Bertrand.

"BIG" JIM GARRISON (RIGHT)
WITH MARK LANE, LAWYER, AUTHOR, AND
CRITIC OF THE WARREN REPORT.

CLAY SHAW (RIGHT) AND HIS ATTORNEY

Nevertheless Garrison seized upon the existence of Clay Bertrand as the vital clue in his case. Oswald was dead. Ferrie had recently died of a cerebral hemorrhage. The only man who remained alive of the three whose conversation had been overheard was the mysterious Bertrand. But no Clay Bertrand could be found.

The case might have bogged down at that point if Garrison had not decided that "Clay Bertrand" was an alias for a prominent New Orleans businessman, whose real name was Clay Shaw. Several factors led Garrison to this conclusion. Both men had the same first name. Both were tall, middle-aged, with thick white hair. Bertrand was described as being fluent in Spanish; Shaw was fluent in Spanish. Bertrand was known to be homosexual; Shaw was homosexual. Finally, Lee Harvey Oswald had been arrested for passing out pro-Castro pamphlets and creating a disturbance at the New Orleans Trade Mart, a commercial development which Clay Shaw had helped build and run. To Garrison's mind, this suggested that Oswald and Shaw may have known each other.

On the basis of this evidence, Garrison had Shaw arrested for conspiracy to murder the President of the United States. The charge was conspiracy, not murder, because Garrison had no evidence that pointed to Shaw as one of the assassins.

News of Shaw's arrest made Garrison famous. He was invited to be a guest on the Johnny Carson show, where he discussed the case at length in spite of a court order forbidding him to do so. He was also granted an interview by *Playboy* magazine, one of the longest interviews in that magazine's history.

Garrison's investigation brought numerous reporters to New Orleans to cover the story. It also attracted a number of the better-known critics of the Warren Commission. For some time, the critics had demanded that the case be reopened so that the truth could be determined. They hoped that Garrison's work would offer a second chance to look at the evidence. Mark Lane, the author of *Rush to Judgment*, enthusiastically endorsed the district attorney's work and stayed in New Orleans to assist in it. Edward Jay Epstein, Richard Popkin, and Harold Weisberg also made their appearance.

In a matter of months, however, Garrison's case began to founder. One of the first attacks on it was made by James Phelan, in a story that appeared in the *Saturday Evening Post*. Phelan went at Garrison from several angles, but his most damaging disclosure, unknown to the general public up to that time, was that Russo had said nothing during his first interview with Garrison's staff about a conspiracy. It was only when he had been given truth serum and placed under hypnosis that Russo told the story leading to the arrest of Clay Shaw. If Russo's testimony had been so important, why had it been forgotten so easily? But more importantly, had suggestions been planted in his mind while he was drugged and unconscious?

After Phelan's story came more revelations, this time by Walter Sheridan of NBC News. Sheridan discovered that Garrison's assistants had attempted to bribe three witnesses in order to get them to testify against Clay Shaw. He found, too, that they had also asked a burglar to break into Shaw's home and plant evidence there that would incriminate Shaw in the conspiracy. If this was the way the district attorney handled the case, Sheridan seemed to be asking, could there be any truth in any of his claims concerning the Kennedy assassination?

But perhaps the decisive deathblow to Garrison's case turned out to be the defendant himself. After his arrest, Shaw maintained a dignity and calm that impressed everyone. He simply did not behave like a man responsible for the death of a President of the United States or someone who would associate with people like Oswald and Ferrie. Moreover, Shaw's record spoke for itself. For years he had been active in business and civic affairs in New Orleans, where his talents and activities were widely respected. In 1960, he had supported Kennedy's campaign for the Presidency. He was also known to be a friend to the minorities of New Orleans, particularly the Jews and the blacks. Few people could bring themselves to believe that this man had plotted to kill Kennedy.

Shaw's case did go to court, but soon after it began, the trial turned into a farce and travesty of justice. Garrison rarely appeared in court, leaving the prosecution to subordinates who proved inept and inexperienced. The Zapruder film was shown repeatedly, as though to frighten the jury with its gory scenes. Experts were called who talked about the likelihood that there had been two or more assassins at Dealey Plaza. But all to no avail. Whatever the jury believed had happened at Dealey Plaza was beside the question. They were there to judge whether or not Clay Shaw had participated in a conspiracy, and Garrison's staff offered no real proof of that.

The strongest testimony offered by the prosecution was a group of witnesses from the small Louisiana town of Clinton. The "Clinton people," as the press dubbed them, told the court under oath that they had seen a black Cadillac with three occupants in Clinton in August or September of 1963. The occupants, they said, were Lee Harvey Oswald, Ferrie, and Clay Shaw. Strangers were rare in Clinton, so the men in the Cadillac were easy to remember. The town marshal said that he had talked with the driver of the car, whom he identified as Shaw. Oswald had gotten a haircut, according to a local barber. Others remembered seeing the three men sitting in the Cadillac and were positive in their identifications.

Here were several disinterested witnesses who seemed to offer proof that Ferrie, Oswald, and Shaw had known one another. Yet there was a problem. The Clinton people admitted that they had been brought by Garrison's aides to the courtroom days before they were to testify. At that time, Shaw had been pointed out to them as the man under trial. Had this action caused them to be prejudiced against Shaw? Would they have so readily identified him as the man they had seen in Clinton if they had seen him for the first time when they went to the witness stand?

Most of the other prosecution witnesses failed to help Garrison's case against Shaw, and many actually did damage to it. Perry Raymond Russo, on whose testimony so much of the case depended, was one of the worst witnesses. When he took the stand, it was already widely known that he had failed a lie-detector test administered by Garrison's staff on the very material he would be questioned about in court.

Shaw's lawyers were merciless. They made Russo admit that the conversation he claimed to have overheard at Ferrie's apartment had been nothing but an inconsequential "bull session," with no serious import. They likewise made him concede that Ferrie was a talker, and that it was not always possible to take his talk seriously.

Shaw's lawyers then put a New Orleans policeman on the stand who had talked with Russo outside the courtroom. The policeman testified that Russo had been so angered by questions that Shaw's lawyers had asked him earlier in the trial that he told the policeman he

PERRY RAYMOND RUSSO
ARRIVES TO TESTIFY AGAINST CLAY SHAW.

would be willing to lie under oath, if it meant that Shaw's lawyers would lose their case. With that testimony, Garrison's prosecution lost any force it might still have had. If the star witness against Shaw was so willing to lie in court, why should anything he happened to say be taken seriously?

Some of the remaining prosecution witnesses invited laughter or total disbelief. One appeared in court wearing a toga and declared himself to be Julius Caesar. Another claimed that he was the victim of a plot on the part of his former psychiatrist and the New York Police Department, who were trying to hypnotize him and drive him out of business. How do you know the police are trying to hypnotize you, the man was asked. If someone tries to catch your eye and then stares at you, "that's a clue right off," he replied.

The jury took less than an hour to return a verdict of not guilty. Shaw was set free, to the relief of his many friends and others throughout the country who had followed the case. The tireless Garrison attempted to re-arrest Shaw and to bring charges of perjury against him, but a federal court stepped in. In the following years, Garrison was indicted for income-tax evasion and other crimes, but was acquitted of all the counts against him. Finally, in 1973, he lost reelection to the post of district attorney and returned to the private practice of law.

The chief victim of the trial in New Orleans was Clay Shaw. Garrison's accusations severely disrupted his life and forced him out of retirement into a position of national notoriety that he hated and found deeply painful. Even his acquittal brought him little relief or satisfaction. Facts about his personal life were now public knowledge and he was irrevocably connected in the mind of the public with the whole sordid affair.

But there were also other victims of the district attorney's grotesque effort to blame Shaw for the assassination. The critics who flocked to New Orleans to assist Garrison found themselves discredited. Garrison had announced to the world that he had solved the assassination. Mark Lane, Richard Popkin, and other important critics had echoed his certainty and had given him their congratulations on a job well done, before the case had come to trial.

The Garrison trial challenged the credibility of the critics, just as the critics themselves had undermined the credibility of the Warren Report. If the critics— the men and women who had devoted so much study to the assassination—could be misled and fooled, did they really know anything about Kennedy's death unknown to the rest of us? Why accept their attacks on the Warren Report, when they could be deceived so easily by a flamboyant and dishonest district attorney?

The critics reacted in two ways to the discredit brought on them by the Garrison fiasco. First, some of them attempted to salvage the more valuable parts of the collected research. Garrison hadn't been all wrong, they argued. He was on the right track in some instances, but these had been cast aside because of all the mistakes he had made. Why, for instance, had the Clinton people been able to identify Oswald, Ferrie, and Shaw as the men they had seen in their town? There was nothing they had to gain by making the story up or by lying under oath.

Perhaps the Clinton people had recognized Oswald and Ferrie, but had made a mistake in their identification of Clay Shaw. Instead of Shaw, perhaps they had seen W. Guy Bannister, the former FBI agent whose name had been mentioned in association with Ferrie and Oswald. Bannister was said to have looked something like Clay Shaw, but since he had died before Shaw's trial began, he could not be brought to court. If Bannister had been brought to trial instead of Shaw, the critics argued, the truth might have been discovered.

The second way some of the critics reacted to the Garrison affair was to believe that the trial itself had been part of a cover-up. The CIA, the Cuban exiles, or whatever group had been responsible for the assassination may have planted evidence that misled the district attorney and caused him to go off in the wrong direction. Or perhaps Garrison—who had often been accused of involvement with Mafia figures—was himself responsible for the charade, in order to draw attention away from his friends and put a stop to any investigation that might lead to the Mafia. In either case, the result had been the same. The critics and their findings had been made to look foolish and unreasonable. And since no one had gained more from this state of affairs than those genuinely guilty of the murder, it was easy to conclude that they had been the ones who arranged the trial and the whole set of events surrounding it.

The critics had hoped that the Garrison investigation would provide a second chance for an official inquiry into the assassination. It would replace the Warren Report and settle all the problems that report had failed to answer. Instead, the trial in New Orleans set back the work the critics hoped to accomplish by several years. The public had heard enough discussion for a while about the Kennedy assassination, particularly when that discussion seemed to lead nowhere.

But the indefatigable critics—men such as Mark Lane and Bernard Fensterwald—continued to demand that a new investigation be set up. The truth, they believed, was there to be found. Pessimists and skeptics thought differently and argued that too much time had passed and that nothing could be learned now that was not already known. Tragically, what led eventually to the establishment of a new commission to study the Kennedy assassination were the assassinations of two other gifted American leaders, Martin Luther King, Jr., and Robert F. Kennedy. It is now time to look at these other political murders and see how they, too, became clouded in mystery and uncertainty.

Section Two

The Assassination of Dr. Martin Luther King, Jr.

MARTIN LUTHER KING, JR., 1929–1968

Chapter Six

THE BACKGROUND OF THE ASSASSINATION

In Memphis, Tennessee, the months of February and March 1968 were tense and troublesome. For more than a year the city authorities had feared that racial strife might break out between whites and blacks, and now they believed there was genuine cause for alarm. On February 12, the sanitation workers had gone on strike for better wages and better working conditions. For the most part black and poor, they were tired of low pay and backbreaking work. Moreover, they felt victimized by a city that gave them no job security and no insurance. If they were hurt or killed while at work —as two of their number had been on February 1— there was no worker's compensation to help their families overcome the loss of income. The sanitation workers wanted a better life for themselves and announced that they were willing, if necessary, to fight for it.

Henry Loeb III, the mayor of Memphis, promptly decided to take a hard line against the strikers. A strike by municipal employees, he said, was illegal and could never be condoned. He refused to negotiate with the leaders of the strike and demanded that the men return to their jobs or face severe penalties. Ten days after the strike began, the city hired nonunion workers to pick up the garbage and sent police cars to accompany the trucks as they made their rounds.

The mayor was a stubborn man who believed it was enough that he had the vast majority of Memphis whites behind him. He expected that the sanitation workers would be forced to capitulate after a short time and that things would then return to the way they had been before the strike. What the mayor did not realize was that the blacks of Memphis had developed a new sense of unity and determination and that they were now under the able leadership of the Reverend James M. Lawson, Jr., pastor of the Centenary Methodist Church.

By any standards, Reverend Lawson was an unusual and talented man. A devout Christian, he had long put his faith into action. During the Korean War, he had spent time in prison because he believed that a Christian should never kill another human. As a missionary in India during the mid-1950s, he had become a disciple of the teachings of Mahatma Gandhi, the great Hindu leader. Gandhi had developed the doctrine of nonviolence as a means of overcoming the British occupation of his country. Lawson came to believe that the same doctrine could be used in the United States to awaken the conscience of the nation and put an end to racism.

It was in India that Lawson first heard of the Reverend Martin Luther King, Jr. Dr. King, who was pastor of the Dexter Avenue Baptist Church in Montgomery, Alabama, had become known throughout the world when he successfully led a long and difficult boycott to integrate Montgomery's public transportation system. As a result, blacks were no longer forced to sit in the back of the bus and they no longer had to give up their seats to whites on demand.

But what interested Reverend Lawson most about the boycott was that King had put into action the very principles of nonviolence Lawson had come to admire in India. King had taught his followers to accept the violence inflicted on them but never to return that violence. He had shown that the racist laws which kept black people in an inferior position in American society could be overturned, if blacks simply and courageously refused to abide by them.

When he returned from India, Reverend Lawson visited King and the two became close friends. They worked together in the Southern Christian Leadership Conference (SCLC), which King had established in 1957 to coordinate his nonviolent program. Over the years, Lawson and King had faced many hardships together. Their lives had frequently been threatened and together they had seen the ugliness that racism could arouse among whites who were angered by the demands of blacks for equality and improved conditions.

As Reverend Lawson attempted to unify the blacks of Memphis that February and to give support to the sanitation workers, his thoughts turned toward Dr. King. He believed King's presence in Memphis was needed. Reverend King would help boost the morale of the city's black people, but more importantly, a man of his reputation would force the mayor and city council to take notice that the blacks were determined to win the strike. With this in mind, Lawson got in touch with his friend and asked him for assistance.

That spring, Reverend King and his staff happened to be very busy. For months they had planned and carried out a campaign against poverty that was to culminate in Washington, D.C., on April 30, with a "Poor People's March." The success of this campaign was very important to Dr. King. He wanted to dramatize the plight of America's numerous poor people—both black and white—and to urge the federal government to take action that would better their situation.

King wanted the campaign to be successful for another reason. In recent years, his doctrine of nonviolence had come under attack by younger, more militant black leaders, who believed that violence was the only way to change the racist American system. King hoped that a successful nonviolent campaign against poverty would help to vindicate the idea of nonviolence and discredit the more militant blacks. Violence would only lead to more violence, he believed, and if American blacks began to use force against the whites, they would be sowing the seeds of their own destruction.

Dr. King realized that a trip to Memphis would cut into an already busy schedule. Some other event that had already been planned would have to be sacrificed. But Memphis, he reasoned, was important. The strike involved the plight of poor people in a very real way, and he couldn't very well ignore it while professing to take up their cause. He told Lawson that he would come and do what he could to help.

On March 18, King made his first appearance in the troubled city. He spoke before an audience of more than fifteen thousand and was so moved by its display of unity, confidence, and determination that he promised to return in four days. At that time, he said, he would lead one of the daily marches that were taking place in support of the sanitation men. He called for a general strike, a strike that would bring the whole city to its knees. "I want you all to stay home from work that day," he said. "I want a tremendous work stoppage, and all of you, your families and children, will join me and I will lead you in a march through the center of Memphis."

The crowd readily accepted King's challenge and the next few days were spent in preparation for a major confrontation with the mayor and city council. On March 22, however, an unusually heavy snowfall began to cover Memphis, the second biggest snowfall in the city's history. The march was postponed to the 28th.

The extra week provided additional time for preparation but did not avert what turned out to be a disaster for Dr. King. Black anger and resentment had grown considerably since the strike began, almost two months earlier. There had been too little time to train people in the doctrine of nonviolence, too little time to explain the sort of courage it took to face one's enemies without hatred or without wishing to do them harm. Many Memphis blacks wanted a fight or at least some way to vent the rage they had come to feel.

When the march began on the morning of the 28th, it quickly got out of hand. A few of the demonstrators broke ranks and began to smash shop windows. The Memphis police had stayed out of sight so as not to provoke the crowd, but now they stepped in. One black was killed, sixty beaten, and three hundred arrested before order was restored.

Dr. King and his chief aides managed to escape, but King was deeply depressed by what had happened. He returned to his room at the Lorraine Motel to consider what to do next and how to repair the damage that had been done. Everything he had feared might happen had indeed taken place. Nonviolence had turned to violence, and his leadership had been ignored by militant blacks —the ones who had thrown stones at the shop windows. In the national press, editors and reporters wondered if Dr. King had lost control of the movement and if he would be able to restrain the actions of the militants in the future.

King's depression, however, was short-lived. Never a quitter, his experiences over the previous decade had strengthened the fighter in him and he determined that he would win in Memphis. He rallied the support of de-

THE MARCH OF THE STRIKERS TURNS VIOLENT,
AND POLICE MOVE IN TO BREAK IT UP.

voted followers—men such as Ralph Abernathy and Andrew Young—who had worked with him for years. On April 3 Dr. King held a press conference at the airport and announced that he would lead a *nonviolent* march on April 8. This time, he said, he would make certain that the demonstration would not end in violence. It would be a display of unity among the blacks of the city and would show their determination to win higher wages and better workers' benefits for the sanitation men.

That evening, Dr. King made a speech before a huge audience assembled at the Mason Temple. He told them that it was their duty to see that the mistakes of the 28th were corrected. He then turned the talk to his own personal feelings and experiences. He said that he believed himself to be particularly blessed to live in the second half of the twentieth century, a time God had chosen to be of great importance. "Something is happening in our world," he declared, "something of utmost significance. We must see that the doctrine of nonviolence prevails, because we have no other choice. It is nonviolence or nonexistence. All of us must learn to live together in peace and love, or we will eventually destroy one another."

King spoke of the assassination attempt against him in 1958, when a demented woman had stabbed him with a letter opener. The blade, he said, had come dangerously close to his aorta—a matter of an inch or two (2.5 cm), and he would have died. Threats against his life had been made many times and had already been made in Memphis. "We've got some difficult days ahead," he reminded his listeners.

He paused and then began to speak with unforgettable eloquence. It was a speech he had given before, but this evening it was particularly moving. The threats against his life no longer bothered him, he said, "Because I've been to the mountaintop. Like anybody I would like to live a long life. But I'm not concerned about that now. I just want to do God's will. And He's allowed me to go to the mountaintop. And I've looked over—and I've seen the Promised Land. So I'm happy tonight, I'm not worried about anything, I'm not fearing any man. Mine eyes have seen the coming of the Lord."

The next day was filled with the petty problems and negotiations necessary to any major undertaking. Meetings had to be held with the leaders of the various black organizations in Memphis. City officials had to be met with and convinced that they should allow the march to take place. On top of it all, there was the Poor People's March in Washington, now only three weeks away, with problems of its own that had to be ironed out. Dr. King was worried that he would not find the time to do everything that needed to be done.

The evening, however, was to be a time of rest and relaxation. King and a few of his closest friends had been invited to a soul food dinner at the home of the Reverend Samuel Kyles, the pastor of the Monumental Baptist Church in Memphis. Reverend King looked forward to the evening all day. Toward dinnertime, his spirits began to lift. He joked with his assistants and assumed a less serious, less restrained mood.

As it neared six o'clock, most of King's aides were already in the Lorraine Motel parking lot waiting to leave. Ralph Abernathy, his closest friend, was still in his room, and the Reverend Kyles was waiting on the motel balcony not far away. As Abernathy slapped some aftershave on his face, King walked out onto the balcony to talk to his aides, who were standing by the cars below. He stood for a few minutes on the balcony, leaning against the railing. Solomon Jones, King's chauffeur,

TWO OF DR. KING'S CLOSEST AIDES AND FRIENDS,
RALPH ABERNATHY (LEFT) AND ANDREW YOUNG.

THE LORRAINE MOTEL,
SCENE OF THE SHOOTING OF DR. KING.

noticed that the evening was growing chilly and suggested that King take a coat. As Dr. King turned to go back into his room, a single shot rang out. In the parking lot below, the aides fell to the ground, fearing that other shots might be fired. Reverend Kyles ran to King and saw that he had been wounded in the right jaw, and that he already had lost a great deal of blood. Kyles then ran to a phone to try and get an ambulance, but the sight had made him hysterical and he was not able to get himself under control. Ralph Abernathy was the next man to reach Dr. King. When he got there and saw the fright in his friend's eyes and noticed the horrible wound, Abernathy took King into his arms and tried to comfort him.

Seconds after the rifle shot, the Memphis police were at the Lorraine Motel. Unknown to Dr. King, who had refused special police protection because it conflicted with his doctrine of nonviolence, a policeman had been stationed at a nearby fire station to keep an eye on the motel. At 6:01, this policeman had heard the single shot and had seen King fall backward. Immediately he had sent out an alarm for help and assistance. At the same time, a fireman at the station had ordered an ambulance.

Everyone who had been nearby when it happened agreed that the shot had come from the area in back of a run-down two-story red-brick building about two hundred feet from the Lorraine Motel. But there was disagreement as to whether the shot had come from the building itself or from the bushes at its base. Solomon Jones claimed to have seen a man in the bushes below the building only seconds after the shot had been fired. Others believed it had come from a second-story window that was partially open and which provided a convenient view of the balcony King had been standing on.

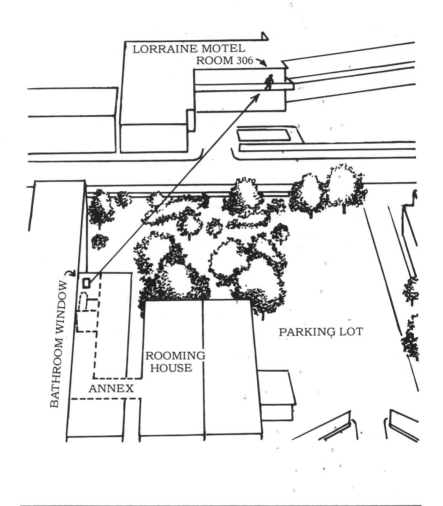

LORRAINE MOTEL
ROOM 306

BATHROOM WINDOW

PARKING LOT

ROOMING
HOUSE

ANNEX

GENERAL LAYOUT OF THE AREA.

BATHROOM
WINDOW

ROOMING HOUSE AS SEEN
FROM THE MOTEL BALCONY.

Lieutenant J. E. Ghormley, one of the policemen who rushed to the scene of the crime, realized that if the assassin had been in the building, his or her best route of escape would have been from its front entrance. This entrance faced onto Main Street and could not be seen from the motel. Ghormley rushed around to Main Street, but could see no one. Perhaps the assassin was still in the building. As he walked down the street toward its entrance, Ghormley passed the Canipe Amusement Company. What he saw caused him to stop short. In the doorway of a store there appeared to be an old green bedspread lying in a heap with something jutting out from it—6 or 7 inches (15 cm) of a rifle barrel.

At that moment Guy Canipe, the owner of the store, came out of the front door and told the lieutenant that the package had been dropped there only moments before. It had been left by a youngish white man, he said, who appeared to be in a great hurry. After he had deposited the package, the man had run to a white Mustang and driven away. Ghormley relayed this information to police headquarters, where the first description of the suspected assassin was released at 6:08, only seven minutes after King had been shot. "Suspect described as young white male, well-dressed, believed in a late-model white Mustang, going north on Main from scene of shooting." Ghormley remained at Canipe's to guard the evidence.

Meanwhile, other policemen ran into the building from which the shots seemed to have been fired. It was a cheap boardinghouse, which catered to people on small incomes. The first policeman to reach the second floor was directed to room 5B by one of the tenants. He found evidence that someone had recently been in the room, but a quick glance through the room's window made him realize that the shot could not have been fired

(100)

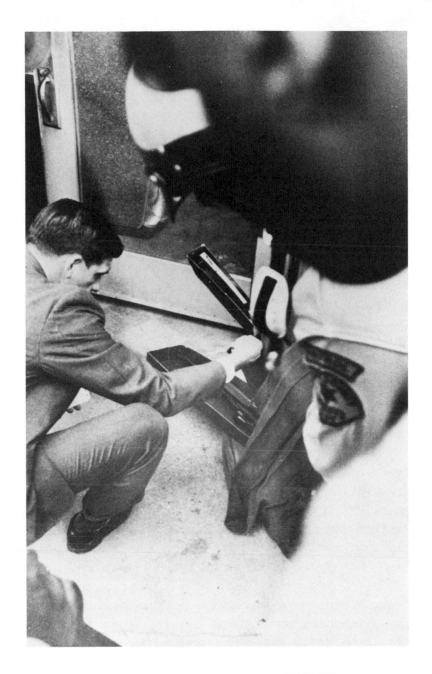

POLICE FIND THE MURDER WEAPON
JUST MINUTES AFTER THE SHOOTING.

from there. To have hit Dr. King from that angle would simply have been too difficult.

The police then went down the hallway to the bathroom, which was shared by several people who lived in the boardinghouse. The bathroom window was open and afforded an excellent view of the Lorraine Motel balcony. There were scuff marks in the old-fashioned bathtub, perhaps made by the shoes of the assassin as he stood in the tub to look out the window. On the wall by the tub was a blurred palm print, where he may have steadied himself.

Two roomers, Charlie Stephens and Willie Anschutz, told the police they had seen a man leaving the boardinghouse in a hurry. He had been carrying a long, narrow package under his arm. Both roomers said they had been irritated because the man had monopolized the bathroom all afternoon, but had not run water or flushed the toilet, so that there was no indication of why he spent so much time there. Stephens, who was to become one of the most important witnesses in the case, had seen the new boarder up close when they passed in the hallway. Anschutz had seen him only indistinctly.

The police learned from Mrs. Bessie Brewer, the manager of the boardinghouse, that the man in 5B was a John Willard who had checked in about 3:30 that afternoon. Mrs. Brewer described him as in his early thirties, neatly dressed, and clean. She had been impressed with him, because her usual boarders were people who had long since ceased caring about their appearance.

The police sealed off the bathroom and room 5B and began to examine them closely. They took charge of the rifle, binoculars, and personal effects found wrapped in the green bedspread. The assassination of President Kennedy was still fresh in everyone's memory, and the Memphis police did not want accusations of carelessness and negligence hurled at them as they had been hurled at the Dallas police five years earlier. Still less did the Memphis police want to be considered as accomplices of the assassin or in any way responsible for his not being brought to justice.

Meanwhile, Dr. King had been taken to St. Joseph's Hospital. A team of doctors, including a neurosurgeon, was assembled to work on him, but with no success. King was officially declared dead at 7:05 p.m., Memphis time, a little more than an hour after he had been shot. The bullet had pierced his chin and neck and had severed the spinal column, doing considerable damage to the brain. If he had lived, Dr. King would have been paralyzed from the neck down, except for his arms, and his once-eloquent voice would have been severely impaired.

King's death unleashed the anger of blacks throughout the country. In riots that followed the news of his murder, thirty people were killed and scores injured. An estimated $30 million worth of damage was done to property. Few major cities were spared at least some form of violence. It was one of the darkest days in recent American history. At his funeral a few days later, many prominent people from all walks of life assembled to pay their respects to this most unusual man.

Dr. King had long prophesied that he would die by violence. He had warned his family and friends about this, and had himself come to an acceptance of what he saw as his fate. King's Christian faith had helped him to recognize evil and the human capacity to do harm and injury. But that same faith had sustained Dr. King and made him great.

Perhaps more than any other event, King's life and assassination are a comment on our times. They reveal something of the extent of human goodness and human greatness. They also reveal something of the extent of human evil.

Chapter Seven

THE SEARCH FOR THE ASSASSIN

The search for the killer of Martin Luther King, Jr., began shortly after the assassination and became one of the most extensive manhunts in history. More than 3500 FBI agents were involved, along with the police of Memphis and the police of a dozen foreign nations. In the end, the investigation would cost more than $1 million and consume a great deal of time and effort. But for Attorney General Ramsey Clark, head of the Department of Justice, it was worth the price. Clark believed that those responsible for the murder of Dr. King had to be caught and brought to trial. There could be no lingering doubts about the assassination, no suggestion of a cover-up, no feeling that the government had failed to do its job.

The FBI and the Memphis police had substantial evidence with which to start their investigation. The manager of the boardinghouse and two of its tenants had seen the suspect and could describe him. Several people had noticed the white Mustang and some had seen a man drive away in it shortly after the assassination. But most importantly, the police had the evidence the assassin had left behind in the doorway of the Canipe Amusement Company. Wrapped in the old green bedspread, they had found a Remington 30.06 rifle with telescopic sights, a pair of binoculars, and several cartridges. They had also found an overnight bag that contained personal belongings, including a pair of pliers, deodorant, toilet paper, soap, and beer. The police also had in their possession a pair of underwear shorts and a white T-shirt, both with a laundry mark 02B-6 attached to them in black letters on white tape.

Soon after it started, the investigation began to bear fruit. The first clue to be identified was the pliers, which had been purchased from a store in Los Angeles. Then came the rifle. The FBI traced its serial number and learned that it had been sold by the Aeromarine Supply Company in Birmingham, Alabama, on March 30, only five days before the assassination. The purchaser had listed his name as Harvey Lowmyer. Further investigation revealed that a man answering Lowmyer's description had visited several gun shops in the Birmingham area in late March. He had asked questions about different kinds of guns, including their range, trajectory, and how far a bullet could be expected to drop when fired from a certain distance. Moreover, the description of Lowmyer offered by the store clerks in Birmingham fit the description of John Willard given by the people who had seen him in Memphis.

The laundry marks on the underwear and T-shirt were the next clues to be identified. FBI agents had scoured Memphis, looking for the place where they had been laundered, but had turned up nothing. Finally, on April 11, the marks were traced to the Home Service of Los Angeles, California. The number had been assigned to an Eric S. Galt and had been stamped on the clothes sometime in mid-March. Since Dr. King had been in Los Angeles at that time, the FBI assumed that Galt had followed King to Los Angeles, perhaps to kill him there, but had missed his opportunity.

On the same day that the origin of the laundry marks was discovered, the name Eric Galt appeared a second time in the investigation, on the other side of the country. A resident of the Capitol Homes section of Atlanta, Georgia, a housing project for low-income families, reported an abandoned white Mustang that had been parked for several days near the apartment. When FBI agents took charge of the automobile, they found that it was registered to Eric Starvo Galt and that Galt had given his residence as Birmingham, Alabama.

A careful search of the car showed that threads and hair found in the trunk and on the floor were identical with those found in room 5B of the boardinghouse in Memphis. The strands of hair likewise matched the hair taken from the hairbrush that had been found wrapped in the green bedspread. Furthermore, the description of Galt given by the man who owned the apartment in Birmingham where Galt lived matched the descriptions the FBI had of Harvey Lowmyer and John Willard. The FBI was now certain that Galt, Lowmyer, and Willard were the same person and Eric Starvo Galt, which was assumed to be the assassin's real name, was placed on the bureau's list of the ten most-wanted fugitives.

Other news of Galt came pouring in. In Los Angeles, a cocktail waitress, Marie Martin, and her cousin, Charlie Stein, told investigators that they knew Galt fairly well. Marie had known him as a taciturn and shy customer in the bar where she worked. Charlie had driven to New Orleans with him. In exchange for the trip to New Orleans, where Charlie had family matters to take care of, Galt had asked that Charlie and Marie register to vote in California for George Wallace. Galt was an avid supporter of Wallace, they said, and believed that Wallace was the one man who would defend the rights of white people.

The information supplied by Marie Martin and Charlie Stein led to other discoveries about Eric Galt. On one occasion in Los Angeles, he had fought with a waitress over some black people who were demanding equality and he had also made some strongly racist remarks. Bystanders had to separate him from the waitress when he grabbed her and threatened to take her to a black area and abandon her there "to see how she liked that." The FBI learned, too, that Galt had taken courses in ballroom dancing and bartending while he was in Los Angeles. Agents interviewed instructors at both schools for more details and were rewarded with a photograph of Galt in bow tie, white shirt, and jacket, taken on March 2, 1968, when he graduated from the International School of Bartending. It was the best lead to date.

But the clue that led the police to the true identity of Eric Galt came from another source. In an effort to learn more about the activities of their suspect, the FBI checked every money order that had been cashed in the Los Angeles area during the time Galt had been there. From this survey, the bureau learned that Galt had taken a correspondence course with the Locksmithing Institute of Bloomfield, New Jersey. He had begun the course almost a year earlier, on July 17, 1967, listing his home as Montreal, Canada. The most recent address listed with the school was 113 Fourteenth Street, Atlanta, Georgia—and the address had been sent to them only a few days ago.

When FBI agents in Atlanta went to the address, they found a wealth of information and clues. Galt's landlord identified the man in the bartender's photograph as his tenant, but said he had not seen the man for several days. In the suspect's room, they found a map of Atlanta with Dr. King's church and home circled in pencil. More importantly, however, they discovered

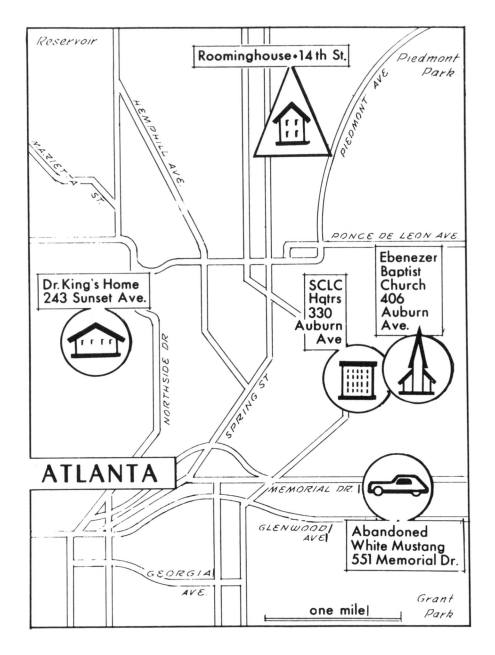

A FACSIMILE OF THE MAP
FOUND IN RAY'S ROOM IN ATLANTA.

a left thumbprint on the map, the first clear and distinct print they had come across. On April 18, FBI print experts began to compare the print with others in their files. They planned to examine the prints of every white male under fifty—a total of more than 53,000 sets of prints.

By the morning of the next day, however, the print experts had identified their man. His prints were on the 700th card examined. He was James Earl Ray, a small-time thief who had escaped from Missouri State Penitentiary nearly a year earlier, on April 23, 1967. Missouri authorities had thought so little of him that they had put out a reward of only $50 for his capture. Now James Earl Ray replaced Eric Galt on the FBI's fugitive list. His picture was distributed throughout the country and turned over to the Canadian police, since Ray, under the name of Galt, had first enrolled in the locksmithing course from Montreal.

As the FBI delved into Ray's past, a more complete picture of the alleged assassin began to emerge. Ray was forty, but looked younger and kept in shape through exercise and weight lifting. He had been born on March 10, 1928, in Alton, Illinois. His father, Jerry, was poor, unable to hold a steady job, and had served time in prison for larceny. His mother Lucille, early in her marriage, had been a hardworking woman who had tried to keep her large family together, even after her husband abandoned her for another woman. The odds against her, however, had been too great. She had become an alcoholic and was frequently arrested for public drunkenness.

Unhappy and poverty-stricken families often produce criminals. Only two of the nine Ray children, Carol and Suzy, matured into responsible adults. The others displayed a variety of emotional and psychological problems. James Earl Ray and two of his younger brothers, John and Jerry, had begun their criminal activities as young men. Each had been repeatedly in and out of jail for burglary and petty theft.

Jimmie, as his family called him, was first arrested in Los Angeles for stealing a typewriter. A few years later, in Chicago, he was sent to prison for two years for armed robbery. In 1955, he was sentenced to three years in Leavenworth, for having forged money orders, and in 1959, he received twenty years—under the Habitual Criminal Act—for the burglary of a grocery store in St. Louis. It was while serving this last sentence in the Missouri State Penitentiary that he escaped, after two previous attempts had ended in failure.

But the best picture of James Earl Ray came from Walter Rife, an ex-convict who had known Ray since they were both fourteen and who had served time with him at Leavenworth. Rife described Ray as a man who regularly broke into houses looking for things of value he could sell. He robbed drunks. He broke into safes and staged armed holdups. Rife could not believe, however, that Ray killed Martin Luther King. Rife knew that Ray had a deep prejudice against black people and often spoke disparagingly of them, but he said that the Ray he had known was a small-time thief, not a murderer, and not a man who could plan and carry out a big operation.

The first substantial word of Ray's whereabouts after the assassination came from Canada. On April 23, a supermarket manager in Toronto saw a strange man standing in a section of his store reserved for employees. When he approached the man to ask him what he was doing there, the man claimed to be looking for part-time work. The manager told him that the market hired only full-time help, and so the man turned and left. The next day, the manager noticed Ray's picture in *Newsweek* and was certain Ray was the man he had seen.

Two weeks later, in a Montreal hotel, a woman guest found a crumpled piece of paper with three names on it: Martin Luther King, Jr., Rap Brown, and Stokely Carmichael. Each was the name of an important black leader in the United States. The first name on the list, Dr. King's, had been crossed out.

All this led Canadian authorities and the FBI to suspect that Ray had come to Canada to assume a new identity and then escape elsewhere. Canadian passports were easier to obtain than American passports, a fact well-known to American criminals and fugitives. Moreover, the FBI knew that Ray had often spoken with admiration of Rhodesia, the African nation where for a long time a tiny white minority ruled the black majority. Perhaps Ray was on his way to Rhodesia—or already there.

In early May, the Canadian police began a systematic check of all recent passport requests, and on May 20 they found what they were looking for. An alert constable recognized Ray's passport photograph in spite of the glasses Ray had worn to disguise himself. The passport showed that Ray was using the name of Ramon George Sneyd and that he had left Canada on May 6 on a BOAC excursion flight to London. The Toronto-to-London part of his ticket had been used, but the return ticket had not. Ray had made it to London and might have already departed for Africa. Scotland Yard was notified to be on the lookout for a man of Ray's description, using the name Ramon George Sneyd.

On Saturday, June 8, the search came to an end, thanks to a British immigration official who was checking passengers about to board a midday flight to Brussels. The official's suspicions became aroused when he noticed that one passenger had two passports: one which he handed over for examination, the other visible in the pocket of the coat he was wearing. The name on the first passport was Sneyd; on the second, it was Sneya. An airport policeman took Sneyd to a nearby room, where he was questioned and told to wait.

Other officers soon arrived. They treated Sneyd politely and cautiously, so as not to anger him or put him on the defensive. But finally, one of the officers told him that they knew he was an American citizen who was wanted for a serious crime in the United States. Up to that time, Ray did not seem to understand why he had been stopped and questioned. Now he knew. "Oh, God," he said, "I feel so trapped." When he was searched, they found he was carrying a loaded .38 and a timetable of flights to Salisbury, the capital of Rhodesia.

Scotland Yard took Ray into custody and notified American officials that he had been captured. He was granted a court-appointed lawyer and informed of his rights. Evidently he had given some thought to what he would do if captured, for he asked the lawyer to contact three American attorneys, one of whom he would choose to defend him when he returned to the United States. The first was Arthur Hanes of Birmingham, Alabama, a segregationist and conservative who frequently defended whites accused of killing blacks. The other two, F. Lee Bailey and Melvin Belli, were widely known for their dramatic courtroom styles and for the difficult cases they took on. Bailey refused to defend Ray on the grounds that Dr. King had been a personal friend; Belli did not respond at all. Hanes, whose views on race were in many ways similar to Ray's, agreed to take the case.

Ray's return to the United States was carefully planned and carried out. The chief fear in the minds of authorities in Britain and the United States was that someone might try to kill him while he was in transit and vulnerable to attack. Threats had already been made against his life, but the police were primarily concerned with two possibilities. If Ray had been part of a conspiracy, his fellow conspirators would want him dead before he could reveal their identities. If they had gone to the trouble to hire Ray to murder Dr. King, they might go to even greater lengths to see that Ray was silenced. The other people who would want to see Ray dead were those who had loved and followed King. Black leaders had already voiced doubts that the assassin would ever be brought to justice. Angry blacks might take the law into their own hands and see that Ray was executed.

On the night of July 18, 1968, Ray was quietly removed from his cell and taken to a C-135 hired especially to fly him from London to Memphis. The press was not notified, nor did it discover until later that the transfer had taken place. The plane, normally designed to carry 127 passengers and crew, carried only Ray, a doctor, four FBI men, and a small crew, and was to land at Millington Air Force Base near Memphis while it was still dark. Sheriff William Morris, the chief law-enforcement official of Shelby County, would take charge of the prisoner at that point and see that he was safely transported to the jail in Memphis. Morris had taken elaborate precautions. He had told no one what route he planned to take from Millington to Memphis and decided himself only at the last minute. If anyone hoped to ambush Ray after the plane landed in Tennessee, he or she would not learn from Sheriff Morris where to wait.

The operation went smoothly, as everyone had hoped. Ray was taken to the Shelby County jail, where a cell had been reconstructed and modernized just for him.

New steel plates had been installed, plates capable of withstanding heavy arms fire. There was also a new and sophisticated electronic system that would monitor Ray's every move and assure that no unauthorized person would be able to get near him. Altogether, more than $100,000 had been spent on the renovation.

On the morning of July 20, Ray had his first conference with his attorneys, Arthur Hanes and Hanes's son and law partner, Arthur Hanes, Jr. The three men lay whispering on the floor with Ray's private shower running so that they would not be overheard by the electronic equipment installed to protect Ray, but which could also be used to spy on him. The lawyers wanted to hear what Ray had been doing since he escaped from the Missouri State Penitentiary—especially how he had supported himself and how he had come to be in Memphis the day that Dr. King was shot.

The story Ray told his lawyers was sketchy. He refused to be specific about how he had escaped from prison, perhaps because he did not want to reveal the identities of those who had helped him. Once free, however, he had gone to St. Louis and then on to the Chicago area, where he had worked for a while as a kitchen helper at the Indian Trail Restaurant in Winnetka, Illinois. There he had lived frugally, saved his money, and moved on to Montreal. A fellow prisoner, Ray said, had told him that Canada was the best place for a man who wanted to conceal his identity to obtain a passport.

Ray told his lawyers that a French-Canadian sailor he met in Montreal had changed his life. "Raoul" (Ray has never disclosed the sailor's last name) hired Ray to do a series of illegal jobs, which included smuggling heroin into Canada and transporting rare coins and jewels between Mexico and the United States. In exchange for these activities, Raoul had promised financial support, identity papers, and a gift of $12,000 so Ray could start a business of his own.

For the next seven months, Ray continued, he had been under Raoul's influence and guidance. It was Raoul who told him to buy the white Mustang and who gave him the money for it. It was Raoul he contacted in New Orleans when he made the trip from Los Angeles with Charlie Stein. And it was Raoul who sent him to Mexico on several errands. In March 1968, a month before the assassination, Raoul had given him $700 to buy a rifle and ammunition. This rifle, Raoul had explained, would be the first of many they would buy in the United States and then resell in Mexico or Cuba.

After Ray had purchased the rifle, he was to meet Raoul at 422½ South Main Street in Memphis, and there the two men would meet representatives of Mexicans or Cubans interested in the weapons. Ray claimed that he followed these orders faithfully. Soon after he registered in the boardinghouse, there was a knock at his door and Raoul walked in. They talked for a while and then Raoul suggested that Ray go downstairs to a nearby bar and have a beer while he, Raoul, cleaned up. Raoul would meet him at the bar and then they would go to dinner. Ray said that he had complied, but while he was waiting for Raoul to join him he heard a shot. He had become frightened and decided to leave Memphis immediately. Only later did he learn that it was Dr. King who had been killed.

As he considered his client's case and story, Arthur Hanes felt certain that he could get Ray acquitted. Under Tennessee law, the jury had to be convinced beyond a shadow of a doubt that a defendant was guilty, and Hanes believed there were several ways he could plant reasonable doubt in the minds of the jurors. First of all Charlie Stephens, the state's star witness, was an alcoholic. It was Stephens who claimed to have seen Ray in the boardinghouse at the time of the assassination. There was a Memphis taxi driver who was ready to testify that he had seen Stephens a little before the assassination and that Stephens had been so intoxicated he could hardly stand.

Then, too, there was the controversy over where the shot had been fired from. No witness could say with certainty that it had come from the bathroom window. Indeed, there were at least two witnesses who claimed that the shot had come from elsewhere, and one of them, Solomon Jones—who had been King's chauffeur—said that he had seen the assassin in the bushes behind the boardinghouse. If Jones were right—and why should one of Dr. King's followers want to lie?—then Ray would be found innocent of the murder, since no eyewitness testimony could place him in those bushes when King was killed. No, thought Hanes, the jury will never find Ray guilty.

The prosecution, however, was of a different mind. Under the leadership of James Beasley and Robert Dwyer, both assistant attorneys general of Tennessee, the case against Ray was being carefully and painstakingly built up. Their investigative team had examined Ray's life from the time he had been born until his arrest in London. They believed their case to be very strong, strong enough to convict Ray and send him to prison or to his execution.

Beasley and Dwyer had the rifle found in front of the Canipe Amusement Company and could trace it to Ray. They had the underwear with the telltale laundry marks. They had the map found in Ray's Atlanta apartment, with Dr. King's home and church ominously circled and with Ray's clear and distinct thumbprint on it. When they began their research, Beasley and Dwyer believed that Ray had acted as part of a conspiracy. But now they concluded that he had worked alone. They were reinforced in this position when they learned that the FBI, in a separate investigation, had come to the same conclusion.

In September 1968, Arthur Hanes, Ray's attorney, was allowed to inspect the evidence the prosecution had collected. Hanes found it impressive, far more impressive than he had anticipated, and began to doubt that he could get his client acquitted. He asked Ray to be specific about Raoul and about other aspects of his testimony; Raoul, after all, was his chief alibi. But Ray remained evasive and vague. Then Hanes discovered that Ray contradicted himself at times or repeated information that Hanes had supplied him earlier, information Ray tried to pass off as something new or just remembered.

On November 10, two days before his trial was scheduled to begin, Ray decided to drop Hanes and look for a new lawyer. He chose Percy Foreman of Houston, Texas, a man with considerable courtroom experience and ability. Out of more than three hundred of Foreman's clients, only one had been executed. The court accepted Ray's new lawyer and granted him four months to prepare his case. The trial was rescheduled to begin on March 3, 1969.

Foreman came to the case believing, as Hanes, that he might get Ray off on a technicality. He thought he could win by planting reasonable doubt in the minds of the jurors. The time spent with Ray, however, had convinced Foreman that his client was guilty and that there was no way he could plead innocent of the charges against him.

Above all, it was Ray's demeanor that discouraged Foreman. An innocent man would have cooperated with his lawyer and supplied needed facts and information. Instead, Ray said much that struck Foreman as outright fantasy, including his story about the all-important Raoul. Foreman came to believe that Ray could tell him little about Raoul because Raoul simply didn't exist.

When pressed to be straightforward and honest, Ray grew surly. He claimed that he didn't care what happened in the courtroom because no jury in Tennessee would ever convict a white man for the murder of a black man. Ray even seemed to believe that he was something of a hero to the majority of Americans and might eventually be given an award by George Wallace, if Wallace were elected President of the United States.

There was only one thing to do, Foreman concluded, and that was to persuade Ray to enter a guilty plea. If he entered a plea of not guilty and was tried by a jury and found guilty, he would receive the death sentence. A guilty plea at the outset of the trial would save his life and probably result in a sentence of ninety-nine years. At first, Ray met this suggestion with adamant refusal. But eventually Foreman prevailed: Ray agreed to change his plea to guilty and to forego the strenuousness of a long trial.

On Monday, March 10, 1969, Judge W. Preston Battle, Jr., heard the formal plea of guilty. The judge went to great pains to make certain Ray understood what was taking place. To every question the judge put before him, Ray answered that he had full awareness of what his guilty plea implied. He was making his plea voluntarily, he said, of his own free will. When the judge was finished, Tennessee Attorney General Phil Canale stood to make a statement, in which he denied the existence of any conspiracy. A thorough investigation, he announced, had turned up no evidence suggesting that Ray had an accomplice. He assured the court that if he

JAMES EARL RAY PLEADS GUILTY
TO THE MURDER OF DR. KING.

had found any such evidence, he would not have hesitated to make it public. Assistant Attorney General Beasley summarized the state's case against Ray: his possession of the murder weapon, his presence at the boardinghouse, his flight to Canada and Europe. The evidence formed a complete chain, he said, a chain that could not be broken and that proved beyond a shadow of a doubt that James Earl Ray had killed Martin Luther King, Jr.

Judge Battle sentenced Ray to ninety-nine years in prison. But the case did not end there. Three days later, on March 13, Ray wrote a short letter to the judge renouncing his guilty plea and dismissing Foreman as his lawyer. In the years that have passed since then, Ray has continued to maintain his innocence. He claims that an admission of guilt was forced on him by those who wanted someone, anyone, convicted of King's assassination. He has exhausted every legal resource open to him to win a new trial. He has worked with lawyers as different as J. B. Stoner, the racist and reactionary leader of the National States' Rights party, one of America's most conservative political groups, and Bernard Fensterwald, a Washington attorney with impeccable liberal credentials.

Ray has convinced many people that he was indeed cheated out of a fair trial. But to others more familiar with his past, the whole affair sounded like something that had happened before. When he had been arrested one other time, Ray had pleaded guilty, was sentenced, and then claimed innocence. Was his turnabout in Memphis merely a repeat of what he had done before when faced with irrefutable evidence against him? Or was he forced to plead guilty against his better judgment? For nearly ten years the question has been debated and no solution has emerged that is satisfactory to everyone who has looked into the case.

Chapter Eight

CONSPIRACY OR LONE ASSASSIN?

The capture of James Earl Ray and his plea of guilty did not put a stop to public discussion about King's assassination. For many, the search for the assassin had proceeded too secretly. The FBI had given the press few details about the extensive investigation taking place, and there was a widespread impression that the government had little interest in solving the crime. Moreover, it was generally known that J. Edgar Hoover, the head of the FBI, had disliked Dr. King intensely and had considered him a menace to the American way of life. How could such a man be expected to conduct an objective inquiry into Dr. King's murder? Wouldn't the investigation be compromised from the very beginning? These were the questions the critics of King's assassination investigation began to ask and for which they wanted clear and satisfying answers.

And, too, there was the problem of the trial itself. The critics pointed out that it had been very short— only one day in length—and that it gave the appearance of being a cover-up. Why had there been no careful presentation of the evidence against Ray? Why had the attorney general of Tennessee believed it necessary to say there was no evidence of conspiracy? Was he trying to conceal something from the public? Many people recalled the failure of the Warren Commission to lay to rest questions about John Kennedy's death and feared that the same thing was happening with the murder of Martin Luther King, Jr.

Indeed, the possibility that Dr. King had been killed by a conspiracy was never very far from anyone's mind. In the course of his career, King had aroused the anger and hatred of many people. He had spoken out against racial injustice, against poverty, and, in the last years of his life, against the war in Vietnam. Time and time again his life had been threatened. Powerful groups resented his influence and feared that he would lead his people to revolution. Would those in power have hesitated to kill King if they felt he threatened their privileged position?

Furthermore, there was eyewitness testimony that suggested Ray may have had accomplices. Two individuals present at King's assassination claimed that the shot had come from the bushes at the rear of the boardinghouse. Solomon Jones said that he had seen a man with a white cloth over his face run from the bushes after the shot had been fired. Had there been two assassins, one at the bathroom window and a second in the bushes? Witnesses had noticed two white Mustangs parked on Main Street not far from the front entrance of the boardinghouse. Was this a coincidence, or had two identical cars been planted there to confuse witnesses and mislead the police?

Two other questions arose that had not been adequately discussed. The residents of the boardinghouse had identified Ray readily enough, but they had also mentioned seeing a blondish man with sideburns in Ray's room that afternoon. Who was this man? Could he have been the elusive Raoul? Moreover, when the police sent out an all-points warning for the white Mustang, they received a CB message from a man who claimed to have spotted the car and had it in hot pursuit. Yet when the police investigated the tip, they found nothing. Had the message been sent by an accomplice of Ray's to mislead the police and send them off on the wrong track while the real murderer made his escape?

All this seemed to imply that Ray had had help. Perhaps there was more to the case than met the eye. But what convinced critics above all else that there was a conspiracy was an examination of Ray's life during the year prior to the assassination.

First, there was the problem of finances. How had Ray supported himself in the months after his escape from prison? He had bought a car. He had crossed the United States several times and had lived in various cities. He had spent time in Canada and in Mexico. He had paid for courses in locksmithing, bartending, and ballroom dancing. He had purchased an expensive rifle with telescopic sights. He had paid for a round-trip ticket from Toronto to London and then had flown to Lisbon, Portugal, and back again to London. When he was captured, he had been heading for Brussels, with plans to fly eventually to Salisbury, Rhodesia. And in addition to all this, he had managed to support himself from day to day.

Where had all this money come from? There was little reason to believe that he had it when he escaped from prison or that his brothers had given it to him once he was free. The only job he had held was as a low-paid kitchen helper. The critics argued that there was no indication that he had financed himself entirely by robbery and burglary, his usual occupations. If he had not worked or stolen for it, they concluded, the money must have come from an outside source, a source that kept him going as he prepared to kill Dr. King.

Second, there was the problem of Ray's passports and his false identities. How had this second-rate criminal— whose record showed him to be inept and mistake-prone —acquired the skill necessary to forge a new identity for himself and travel abroad? In his earlier years, Ray had never shown an aptitude for good planning. In fact, he had been easy to capture whenever he committed a crime and had never really profited from the career he had chosen for himself. Was this the sort of man who had carefully chosen a new identity in Canada, using the name of a man who was roughly his same age, build, and looks? No, said the critics. It was obvious that Ray had been given help. Someone else had arranged for his Canadian passport and someone else had taken care of his travel arrangements.

One of the critics, Bernard Fensterwald, had two specific questions that he wanted cleared up. The first concerned a photograph that was in the possession of the Committee to Investigate Assassinations, the group Fensterwald had founded to look into the deaths of President Kennedy and Dr. King. The photograph had been taken in Dallas, shortly after Kennedy's assassination. It showed two men on Dealey Plaza accompanied by an FBI agent. The two men had been arrested shortly after the President had been shot. One of them, according to Fensterwald, had been identified as a French-Canadian. Ray had described his friend Raoul as a French-Canadian sailor. Could the man in the photograph be Raoul, Ray's accomplice and chief alibi?

The second question that bothered Fensterwald was the number of men arrested at Heathrow Airport in London on June 8, 1968. There were reports of two passports, one belonging to a Sneyd, the other to a Sneya. Were Sneyd and Sneya the same man or were they two different men? The question was important, because a common practice in espionage circles is the establishment of two individuals with similar names, backgrounds, and identities. One travels openly and draws attention to himself, while the second moves secretly and is the true spy, the man who will carry out the "dirty work."

What concerned Fensterwald above all was whether there had been a connection between King's assassination and the assassination of President Kennedy. If Raoul had been the man in Dealey Plaza, then he may well have been one of the masterminds of both operations. If there had been two men at Heathrow Airport, a Sneyd as well as a Sneya, then the double-identity format may have been used for both crimes—two Rays, as well as two Oswalds. The implications, Fensterwald realized, were sinister. His information could indicate that an assassins' bureau was operating in the United States, an organization that eliminated its political enemies and others whom it considered dangerous to American life.

The critics offered several conspiracies to account for the help they believed Ray had to have received. Ray's first attorney, Arthur Hanes, thought that his client had been the dupe of an international Communist conspiracy. This was likewise the conclusion of William Bradford Huie, a journalist who researched the case and published several articles on it in *Look* magazine. At a news conference, Huie told reporters that the Communists had hired Ray to kill King in order to bring revolution and racial war to the United States. They had hoped that Dr. King's death and the violence it brought about would bring America to its knees and strengthen the cause of world Communism.*

* Huie later changed his opinion and concluded that Ray had acted alone.

A second conspiracy theory argued that Ray had been in the pay of Memphis businessmen. These businessmen had been concerned with the economic impact the garbage collector's strike would have on their city. If the strike succeeded, Memphis would lose money, taxes would go up, and black workers throughout the area would demand similar increases. The best way to destroy the strike would be to kill the man who had emerged as its leader—Dr. King. King's death would put fear into the hearts of black people and force them to limit their demands.

According to a third theory, Dr. King had been killed by black militants who resented his popularity and disagreed with his doctrine of nonviolence. The militants had decided to kill King in order to draw his followers away from moderation and pacifism. Their masterstroke had been the choice of Ray to do the murder. A white racist assassin would arouse the anger and wrath of blacks throughout the nation and push them further into the militant camp.

A fourth conspiracy theory was in many ways the most credible of all. This theory held that Ray had been hired by a small group of conspirators, most likely members of the Ku Klux Klan or supporters of George Wallace. The Ku Klux Klan had long advocated violence against black Americans. It had ridiculed King's success and frequently threatened his life. Ray's own views on race coincided closely with the Klan's views. Ray may have come into contact with Klan members, who realized he could be used to kill King. The idea of a conspiracy has been popular with many people, including Dr. King's closest aides and friends. The authorities in Tennessee had either known the truth all along and had chosen to conceal it, or they had failed to dig deeply enough to uncover the evidence showing conspiracy was there.

In recent years, however, the theory that King was killed by Ray and by Ray acting alone or with the help of his family has gained adherents. For these people, there is no evidence, for example, that shows that Ray had been hired by Communists or that Communists had any real interest in assassinating King. Nor is it likely that a group of Memphis businessmen would hire Ray, realizing that King's death would bring violence and destruction—which is usually bad for business.

The black militant argument, too, was unsatisfactory if examined closely. The militants were rigidly black in their orientation. They distrusted whites and wanted little to do with them. Why would they then hire a white racist to kill a black leader? But more importantly, why would the militants risk the assassination of King? If their connection with his death were discovered, they would lose any success they had had in reaching the majority of black people.

Finally, there was no evidence, only speculation, that supported the theory that Ray had been hired by a small group of Klansmen or Wallace supporters. To be sure, there was probably no way this theory could be proved or disproved. A small, tightly knit group of conspirators could easily keep its activities secret and cover up all traces of its deeds. Its work would never be revealed unless one of its members decided to confess, and this was unlikely to happen because he or she would risk reprisals by fellow conspirators.

The best of the lone-assassin theorists were two journalists, Gerold Frank and George McMillan. For them, it was significant that the rifle that killed King could be traced to Ray and only to Ray. Ray alone could be placed in the bathroom of the boardinghouse, and it was Ray's map that was found to have King's Atlanta home and church circled, as though the owner of the map had followed King's activities for some time and had slowly hatched out a plan to murder him. All this led to one conclusion: that Ray had been the assassin and that he had acted alone.

Nor did McMillan and Frank have any problem with explaining Ray's finances. When you looked at the facts, they said, the mystery disappeared. Ray was a very frugal man. Everywhere he went—Los Angeles, Mexico, Atlanta, Canada, even London and Lisbon—he had lived simply and inexpensively. In fact, he had consistently chosen the cheapest boardinghouses and had bought little in the way of clothes.

Even Ray's most expensive purchases—the Mustang and the ticket to London—could be accounted for. By his own admission, Ray had escaped from prison with $275. He may have had more, for he had a reputation among his fellow prisoners for dealing in drugs. Once out of prison, he may have received money from his brothers. Moreover, Ray's income from robbery had to be taken into consideration. He had admitted robbing a brothel in Canada that had netted him $1,700. Was this the only robbery he had carried out in the year before the assassination? Wasn't it likely that he had regularly supported himself by this means, as he had from the time he was a young man?

Money from these sources could easily have taken care of Ray's few needs. He did not have to resort to payment by a band of conspirators. On the other hand, if he had been in the pay of conspirators, wouldn't he have chosen to live and travel more comfortably? Where was the evidence that he had received any payment for his work? McMillan and Frank asked. The evidence showed that he lived from day to day, getting by on what he had.

The problem of the passports and false identities also posed no problem for the lone-assassin theorists. Ray had known that passports were easy to come by in Canada. He had discussed the subject with a fellow inmate while still in prison. He knew where to go and what to do. Besides, Ray had a tested IQ of 108, a bit higher than average intelligence. He was far from stupid or ignorant. The effort needed to find a new identity and acquire a passport were not beyond his capabilities.

While in Canada, Ray had studied birth records to find white males his own age. He had been careful to use the names of men who were approximately his own height, build, and general looks. And every step of the way, he had sought information and taken the advice of people whose job it was to give advice. His flight to London, for example, was no mystery, even for a man who had no experience at foreign travel. He had gone to a travel agent in Toronto, who had filled him in on all the problems he might encounter. He had not needed the help of professional conspirators to oversee his escape.

Frank and McMillan also believed that King's assassination was in no way related to the assassination of President Kennedy. Fensterwald's Dealey Plaza photograph of the French-Canadian was not Ray's Raoul. Ray's descriptions of Raoul were vague and could fit any number of men. And Fensterwald's second question, the double passports at Heathrow Airport, could easily be explained. In Canada, the passport Ray received had misspelled his false identity, registering it as Sneya. Ray noticed this mistake and when he arrived in

Lisbon, he went to the Canadian embassy and received a new passport, this time with his false name spelled correctly. The embassy had not asked for the second passport to be returned. There had not been two men at Heathrow, as Fensterwald suspected. There had only been one man with two passports.

In the course of their separate investigations, Frank and McMillan came to different conclusions about Ray's motive for the assassination of Reverend King. Both men agreed that Ray had a deep and abiding hatred of black people, which he had expressed many times to friends. They agreed, too, that Ray's entire history revealed a loner and a man who preferred to work alone. Ray simply did not get along well with other people.

But at this point, their theories began to diverge. Frank believed that a large part of Ray's motive had been twisted ambition. He had been a second-rate thief who wanted to make a name for himself. His murder of Dr. King had given him international notoriety and had made him one of the best-known criminals of his time. And this was what Ray had wanted. From the escaped convict for whose capture Missouri authorities had offered only $50, Ray had become one of the FBI's ten most-wanted fugitives. More than a million dollars had been spent in an extensive search for him. A special cell had been constructed in the Shelby County jail for him. James Earl Ray had never been treated so royally as he was after he became known as King's assassin.

For McMillan, however, Ray's motives were more complex and partially hidden even from himself. Ray had come from a home where love was seldom expressed among family members and where the father had abandoned the mother. Dr. King represented a special threat to Ray, because King symbolized the "good" father Ray had lacked as a child. King was an admired leader and a father figure, a man with love and concern not only for his own family, but for everyone. In Dr. King, two important sore points in Ray's life came together and formed a dangerous mixture: first, his deep prejudice against blacks, and second, his feeling of bitterness for never having had a loving home. In killing King, Ray was at the same time murdering a black man and destroying a father figure, a figure who happened to represent everything his own father had failed to be.

The question of whether Martin Luther King, Jr., was killed by a conspiracy or by a lone assassin may never be settled to everyone's satisfaction. Ray still maintains his innocence, but remains vague about the details that might prove his innocence. The elusive Raoul has never been found. In the early spring of 1977, Ray made headlines once again when he escaped from the Bushy Run Maximum Security Prison in eastern Tennessee. For several days, people throughout the world debated whether he had been helped to escape by fellow conspirators in the King assassination. Many public figures wondered openly if those conspirators would now kill him so that the truth behind the death of Dr. King would never be uncovered. Four days after his escape, however, Ray was traced by bloodhounds and found hidden under a pile of leaves.

Soon after his return to prison, Ray gave an interview to *Playboy* magazine. Once again he told the story of Raoul and of Raoul's responsibility for the crime. But the *Playboy* reporters went one step further than earlier interviewers who had talked with Ray. They gave him a lie-detector test. The test showed that Ray was lying when he talked about Raoul and that he was lying when he claimed innocence of the assassination.

This "proof" of Ray's guilt, of course, is inconclusive. No court will allow a lie-detector test to decide a person's guilt or innocence. And Ray himself seemed totally unconcerned with the results, saying that he had been ill the day of the test and that his illness had influenced the results. But the test did underline one constant factor in the case—the split between Ray's outward appearance and his inner life. Ray had impressed his first attorneys, Hanes and Foreman, with his calmness and indifference to the charges against him. It was only after they had come to know him that they had found him to be a bundle of contradictions, a man who would tell one story while believing another and who never revealed his innermost thoughts.

Similarly, the men who administered the lie-detector test found Ray outwardly convincing, while the machine recorded a Ray that was simply not visible to the interviewers. This split between the outward, public Ray and the secretive, hidden Ray remains at the core of the case. Any final solution will probably depend on how honest Ray allows himself to be.

But Ray has practiced a lifetime of deception and is now a middle-aged man. If Gerold Frank is right, and his chief motivation is ambition, Ray may never tell the truth, for by shrouding his actions in mystery he can keep his name in the headlines and keep discussion about the King assassination alive.

Section Three

The Assassination of Robert Francis Kennedy

ROBERT FRANCIS KENNEDY, 1925–1968

Chapter Nine

JUNE 4, 1968:
THE ASSASSINATION

The spring of 1968 was a turbulent period in American history. On March 31, President Lyndon Johnson announced to the nation that he would not seek a second term in office. The announcement gave encouragement to the Republicans—after all, it was nearly impossible for the party out of power to defeat the man who already held the Presidency—but also gave rise to hopes among the ambitious members of Johnson's own party. Who would receive the nomination of the Democrats now that Johnson was out?

There were already two Democrats in the field of aspirants. The first was Senator Eugene McCarthy of Minnesota. McCarthy had earned the name "giant killer" when he nearly defeated President Johnson in the New Hampshire primary election earlier in the year. Indeed, his good showing against the President had been one of the reasons that led Johnson to withdraw. McCarthy opposed the war in Vietnam and believed it should be brought to an end. Johnson defended the war and, as President, had been responsible for its escalation and expansion.

The second Democrat to enter the race was Senator Robert F. Kennedy of New York, the younger brother of the late President. Kennedy had been impressed by

McCarthy's substantial showing in New Hampshire and believed that he might make an even stronger candidate. At forty-two, he was handsome, energetic, charismatic, and widely popular among many groups of voters. His experience in government and politics had been varied. In the 1950s he had served as counsel for various Congressional committees, eventually making a name for himself as a tough, stubborn inquisitor of powerful union racketeers and Mafia figures. His work helped uncover the corrupt relationship between some unions and organized crime, and earned him the lasting hatred of men who had profited from that relationship.

After having served as manager for his brother's successful 1960 presidential campaign, Bobby returned to Washington as Attorney General, the chief official of the Department of Justice. At the same time, he served as the new President's closest friend and most trusted adviser. Bobby Kennedy was an active Attorney General and concentrated the powers of his office on enforcing civil rights laws and becoming involved in other controversial issues. He was also planning a major attack on organized crime in the United States and hoped to limit its power severely.

The assassination of his brother in November 1963 had stunned and momentarily disoriented him. He continued to serve as Attorney General for a while, but he and the new President, Lyndon Johnson, did not like each other. Bobby and his brother had made a strong team; with Lyndon Johnson at the head, his role at the Justice Department and in the President's Cabinet was weakened and curtailed.

Kennedy resigned his office and ran for senator from New York. It was the first time he had run for public office, but he easily defeated the incumbent Republican senator, Kenneth Keating.

During his years in government and politics, Bobby Kennedy aroused the hostility and resentment of many people. He was frequently called arrogant and dictatorial. Some even termed him ruthless and said that a man of his character should never be allowed to possess and wield a great deal of power. But there were many others who admired him and saw him as someone who got things done.

When he decided to enter the presidential campaign of 1968, Kennedy realized he would be taking on a difficult and time-consuming task. Eugene McCarthy had already been in the field for months and had gained a substantial reputation for his intelligence and courage. In addition, there was Hubert Humphrey, Johnson's Vice-President, who would almost certainly be a candidate. Humphrey could count on the support of the people who controlled the Democratic party and who believed the nomination should go to a man who had long been active in party affairs. Bobby Kennedy would have to defeat both McCarthy and Humphrey, and defeat them soundly, to show that he was the logical candidate to face the Republicans in November.

Kennedy and McCarthy first met head-on in the Indiana primary election. Indiana was a Midwestern, conservative state with a sizable black minority, and Kennedy considered it a good test of his appeal to a broad spectrum of the electorate. He won Indiana with 42 percent of the vote, 27 percent going to a disappointed McCarthy, and nearly 31 percent to a candidate with close connections to Hubert Humphrey. One week later, Kennedy also won the primary in Nebraska with more than half the votes cast for Democratic candidates.

But then came Oregon, where he lost to McCarthy by 45 percent to 39 percent. His aides and advisers attempted to comfort him by reminding him that Oregon was a comparatively affluent state, with none of the social or racial problems that plagued the rest of the country. In short, they said, it was the sort of state Eugene McCarthy should have been expected to carry. But the defeat was bitter. It was the first defeat Bobby or his brother John had ever experienced at the polls. And it meant that the next primary, in California, would be all the more important. If he were to get the nomination, Kennedy would have to win in California and win decisively.

Kennedy and his staff redoubled their efforts. He spoke to groups in the San Francisco area. He appeared before crowds of Chicano workers and toured Watts, the black ghetto of Los Angeles. As he moved throughout the state, he talked before professional organizations, suburban housewives—anyone interested in his message. Always aware of the importance of media coverage, he was frequently photographed with his children and his wife, Ethel, who was pregnant with their eleventh child.

Everywhere he went, the crowds were large and enthusiastic. People struggled to see him, to get close to him, to touch him. Once, he was accidentally shoved against the door of his car, thereby chipping a tooth and cutting his lip. Aides and bodyguards tried to protect him, but to no avail. Kennedy enjoyed the people and relished their support and encouragement. It was not his style to remain aloof or to fear close physical contact.

Kennedy's message in California centered on the issues that had brought him into the campaign in the first place. It was time, he said, to end division and ill-feeling in the United States. The wasteful, useless war in Vietnam had to be brought to a close. The energies and resources of the nation should be turned toward the solution of its own problems. Black militants and leftist students should be brought back into the mainstream of American life.

In speech after speech, Kennedy denounced the violence that seemed to have become so much a part of American life. What he said was a variation on a speech he had made two months earlier to a crowd of black people in Indiana and which today is etched in stone on his own grave in Arlington Cemetery. "What we need in the United States," he said, "is not division; what we need in the United States is not violence or lawlessness, but love and wisdom, and compassion toward one another, and a feeling of justice toward those who still suffer within our country, whether they be white or they be black." And he concluded with these words: "Let us dedicate ourselves to what the Greeks wrote so many years ago; to tame the savageness in man and to make gentle the life of the world. Let us dedicate ourselves to that, and say a prayer for our country and for our people."

By election day, June 4, it was obvious that his week's activities had paid off. The polls now showed that he had made significant headway and that he was probably ahead of Senator McCarthy. Bobby and Ethel slept late the day of the election, exhausted by the heavy schedule they had kept since the Indiana primary. Later in the day, Kennedy relaxed and played with his children in the surf near the home where they had been staying. Reports were good. The turnout in black and Chicano areas was high, and this meant that Kennedy might well win by the decisive margin he sought. Toward evening, Bobby and Ethel prepared to go to campaign headquarters at the Ambassador Hotel in Los Angeles, where they would await election returns.

They arrived at the hotel around 7:15 p.m., and learned that the vote count was coming in more slowly than had been expected. The new voter machines in Los Angeles were not working properly and without the Los Angeles vote, no one could tell how well Senator Kennedy was doing. Early returns from northern California had put McCarthy in the lead. More encouraging was an announcement from CBS News. On the basis of a small but "scientific sampling" of voting patterns, the CBS computer gave the election to Bobby—and gave him a substantial margin. The other two networks, however, maintained that it was still too early to make a judgment.

The Embassy Room at the Ambassador was filled with well-wishers and followers anxious to hear Kennedy make a victory statement. The crowd—an estimated 1800—was far too large for safety standards. Security officials tried to move some of the people to other parts of the hotel, where they could hear and see the senator speak on television, but few cooperated. The crowd wanted to see Kennedy, and it wanted to see him in person.

Finally, NBC joined CBS and projected a Kennedy victory. McCarthy was still ahead in the count, but Kennedy had accumulated enough momentum in the Los Angeles area to carry the election. Bobby was elated. Everything had turned out as he had hoped. When he appeared in the Embassy Room around midnight to make his statement, the crowd was triumphant. They shouted their enthusiasm, barely hearing Kennedy as he thanked those who campaigned for him and those who voted for him. He then called for party unity and for all Democrats—whether they had supported Humphrey, McCarthy, or someone else—to rally around him at the convention.

After he finished his speech, Kennedy was to go to

the Ambassador's Colonial Room, where he would answer questions from the press. There were two ways he could leave the crowded room he was in, to the left of the speaker's platform or to the right. No one had planned which exit would be used, but when Kennedy finished his victory statement and signaled that he was ready to leave, an assistant maitre d' who worked for the hotel took him by the arm and led him to the right.

This way led through a kitchen and pantry. As the crowd pressed and shoved to get close to the senator, Kennedy's armed security guard, Thane Eugene Cesar, got separated from his charge. So, too, did Rafer Johnson, an Olympic decathlon winner, and Roosevelt Grier, a huge tackle for the Los Angeles Rams football team, both ardent Kennedy supporters serving as additional bodyguards and aides.

Bobby passed through the double doors that led to the next room. He stopped to shake hands with the kitchen staff, cooks, busboys, and others. "Senator Kennedy was smiling," Juan Romero, a kitchen worker, later recalled. "He held out his hand and I shook it." The room was crowded, with nearly one hundred people cramped into its relatively small space. As he turned and paused to chat with the kitchen staff, a dark, slight young man stepped out from beside an ice machine. He, too, held out his hand as though he wanted it shook. Suddenly, several shots rang out. Confusion followed; later, eyewitness accounts about what had happened were to vary considerably. Some claimed they had heard the young man say something before he fired, others said they had heard nothing. Some said the assassin had been very close to Kennedy, others said he had remained several feet (about .5 m) or more away. A television cameraman said that he had seen a man he

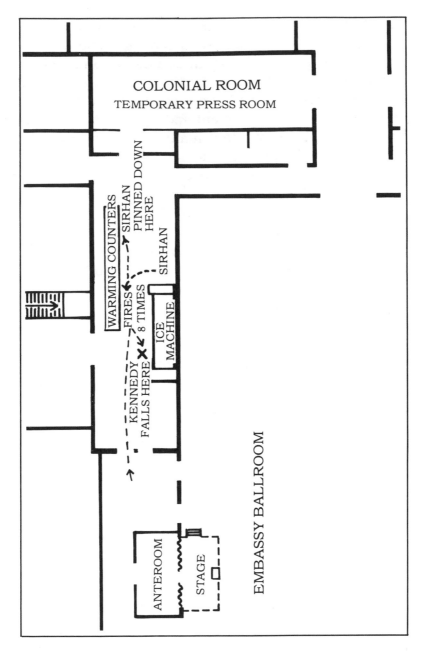

GENERAL LAYOUT OF THE AMBASSADOR HOTEL.

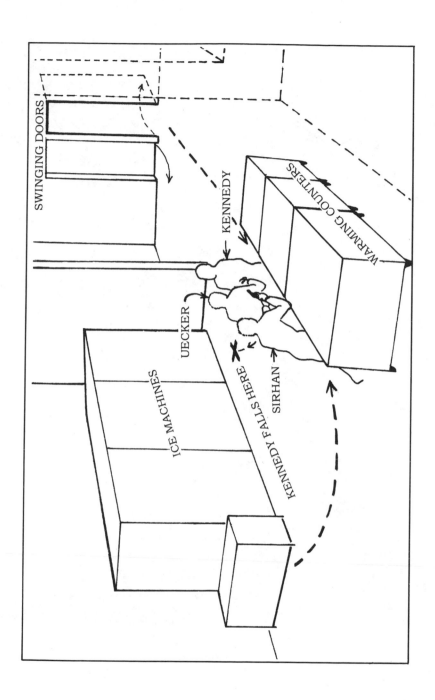

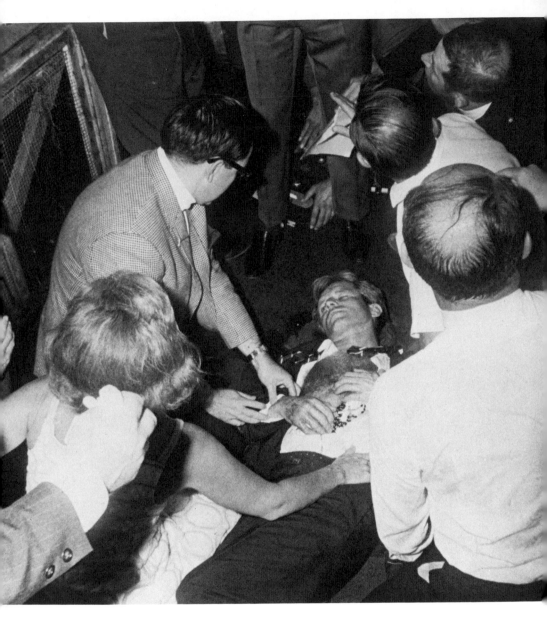

ROBERT KENNEDY LIES
FATALLY WOUNDED ON THE FLOOR.

identified as a security guard fire a gun, but later retracted his testimony. Others claimed they had seen a woman in a polka-dot dress run from the scene as though she had been one of those responsible for the shooting.

Carl Uecker, a hotel employee, was one of the first to reach the young man with the gun and try to restrain him, but at least three more shots were fired before the assassin was finally subdued. Roosevelt Grier, who had used his large body to protect Mrs. Kennedy, lunged for the young man. Rafer Johnson seized his gun. Several bystanders tried to calm the crowd, which wanted to tear the assassin apart. "Let the man live," they said. "We will want to hear his story."

In seconds the scene in the kitchen had been transformed from a celebration to a tragedy. Senator Kennedy lay on the floor, rapidly losing blood. Juan Romero, the kitchen worker, held Kennedy's head while the senator clutched a rosary to his chest. Ethel Kennedy, in far better control of herself than many of the others, found a towel, dampened it, and was at her husband's side trying to ease his pain. In addition to the senator, five others had been wounded, but none as seriously as Kennedy.

Robert Kennedy was taken to Good Samaritan Hospital, where he was declared dead one day later, at 1:44 a.m., on June 6, 1968. Two hours after Kennedy's death, County Coroner Thomas Noguchi performed an autopsy which showed that Kennedy had been struck by three bullets. One had entered behind his right ear and had shattered in the brain. Two others struck in the right armpit. One of these had exited through the right side of the chest, the other had stopped at the base of the neck. A fourth bullet had passed through the shoulder pad of the senator's jacket.

Kennedy's funeral was held at St. Patrick's Cathedral in New York City. Afterward, a train carried his body from New York to Washington, D.C. Thousands of people lined the tracks to pay their last respects. Kennedy was buried in Arlington Cemetery, near the grave of his older brother.

Meanwhile, the young man who had fired the gun in the kitchen pantry had been taken into custody by the Los Angeles police. They had his gun, but more importantly, they had testimony from numerous witnesses who had seen him kill Kennedy. The case against him seemed airtight. No one could foresee that this case, like the cases against Lee Harvey Oswald and James Earl Ray, would soon degenerate into a cloud of doubts and uncertainties.

Chapter Ten

THE INVESTIGATION, CONVICTION, AND UNSOLVED PROBLEMS

The young man taken into custody in the kitchen pantry at first refused to tell the police his real name. He seemed extremely confused and frightened. Many who saw him said he looked as if he were in a trance, perhaps drugged or intoxicated. It was not until the next day that the police learned who he was—Sirhan Bishara Sirhan, a twenty-four-year-old immigrant from the Middle East nation of Jordan.

During the next few days, a portrait of Sirhan began to emerge. He had been born in Palestine on March 19, 1944, and as a child had experienced the growing hostility between the Arabs and Jews of his homeland. His family was very poor and his father had governed his wife and children with a strictness that sometimes became cruelty. He had often beaten his sons harshly and on one occasion had applied a hot iron to Sirhan's foot.

Early in 1957, Sirhan's parents, Mary and Bishara, had immigrated to the United States with their children and settled in Los Angeles. His father, however, did not like America, and within six months had returned to the Middle East, leaving his wife and family behind.

Sirhan learned English and eventually graduated from John Muir High School in Pasadena. His best subjects were the German language and ROTC. Those who knew him at the time have described him as painfully shy, but polite, diligent, and attentive. Sirhan then studied for two years at Pasadena Community College and decided to become a jockey—he was a small man, only 5 feet 3 inches (1.6 m) tall, and it seemed the ideal career.

For several months, Sirhan exercised horses at the Granja Vista Del Rio Horse Ranch in Corona, but a bad fall from a horse in September 1966 forced him to look for something else to do. He moved from job to job. Generally, his employers found him to be hardworking and cooperative and would have liked to see him stay with them. Each time it had been Sirhan's own decision to quit and move on. He seemed uncertain about his future and allowed his life to drift without direction.

But the most important clue to Sirhan's personality was found in his room in the Sirhan family home. There the police discovered a green notebook that had served as a diary, a place where Sirhan had sketched some of his innermost thoughts. Written in poor English and often full of misspellings, the notebook nevertheless revealed much about its author. It showed that Sirhan had planned the assassination for some time.

An entry dated May 18, 9:45 AM—68, a little more than two weeks before Robert Kennedy's death, read: "My determination to eliminate R.F.K. is becoming more the more of an unshakable obsession . . . R.F.K. must die." The deed would have to be done before June 5, 1968, Sirhan wrote. "Kennedy must be assassinated I have never heard please pay to the order of of of of of of of of of of of this or that please pay to the order of." In the next sentence he spoke of the need for a careful plan to solve "the problems and difficulties" of an assassination.

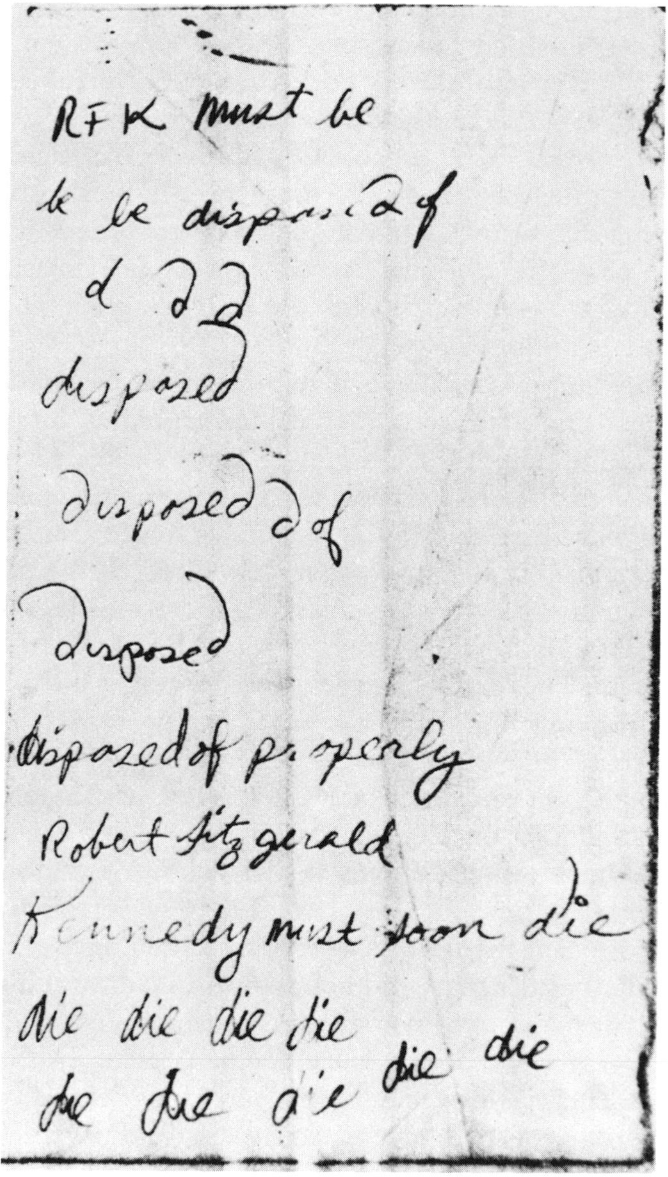

RFK must be

be be disposed of

d 22

disposed

disposed of

disposed

disposed of properly

Robert Fitzgerald

Kennedy must soon die

die die die die

die die die die die

**SIRHAN SIRHAN'S DIARY,
INTRODUCED AS EVIDENCE AT HIS TRIAL.**

The diary revealed little about Sirhan's reasons for wanting Kennedy dead. But it did show that he was full of anger and hatred, both toward powerful American leaders and the United States in general. "The so-called president of the United States of America," he wrote, "must be advised of their punishments for their treasonable crimes against the state moreover we believe that the glorious United States of America will eventually be felled by a blow of an assassins bullet— b bullets bullets."

The diary also showed that Sirhan had brooded over his Arab nationality and that this somehow increased the hatred he felt for the United States and its leaders. In one entry, he expressed a wish for the death of Arthur Goldberg, the American Ambassador to the United Nations and a Jew. "Ambassador Goldberg Must die die on you die die die die me at airport—Sirhan is an ARAB Sirhan you you you you ARAB ARAB you ARAB." The capital letters were perhaps his way of showing how important his Arab heritage was to him.

Sirhan's diary disclosed an individual very different from the Sirhan described by friends, associates, and former employers. Indeed, the diary revealed the secret world of a desperate man, a man whose revolutionary sympathies pushed him toward acts of terrorism and violence. But there was a question on the minds of many people that the diary did not answer: Had Sirhan acted alone or had he been a part of a conspiracy?

Two sections of the diary seemed to imply that he was part of a conspiracy. As we saw in one of the entries quoted above, he had written "please pay to the order of," as though he expected or had already received payment for his deed. In another entry, he had written "moreover we believe that the glorious United States of America will eventually be felled by a blow of an assassins bullet." He had used the word *we*, the first person plural pronoun, as though referring to a group of like-minded individuals who had planned to kill the senator.

There were still other factors that pointed to conspiracy. There was the young woman in the polka-dot dress who had been seen in the pantry of the Ambassador Hotel. The police had sent out a bulletin that described her, hoping to bring her in for questioning, but she has never been found. The problem had been further complicated when it was learned that Sirhan had been seen at a shooting range with a young woman only days before the assassination. The witness who had seen them said it looked as though Sirhan had been teaching her to shoot. Were the woman in the polka-dot dress and the woman at the firing range the same person? If so, this was strong evidence that Sirhan had not acted alone.

In addition, Sirhan's own peculiar conduct after he was captured caused many people to believe he was holding something back, not telling everything he knew. Frequently he was evasive when questioned, and sometimes he was caught lying outright. When asked if he had been paid to commit the assassination, he never replied with a direct yes or no. Instead, he answered, "If I did, where's the money?" Once when asked if he had ever read any books on the assassination of President Kennedy, he said no, but was later tricked into admitting that he had read William Manchester's *The Death of a President* and had collected a shelf of books on the assassination.

Especially mysterious was Sirhan's story concerning his whereabouts on June 3, 1968, the day before the California primary election. He had first told the police that he spent the whole day at home. Then he said that he had gone out driving in the direction of Corona. Later, he boasted that he had driven 350 miles (560 km) on June 3 and that nobody, not even the FBI, could discover where he had been. Was Sirhan trying to hide something? Had he driven the 350 miles (560 km) in order to make contact with his fellow conspirators and arrange last-minute details of the assassination?

Finally, many people were bothered by the trancelike state Sirhan had been in when captured. Sirhan told the police later that he could remember nothing about what had happened in the kitchen pantry. What this suggested to some investigators was that Sirhan had been programmed to kill Kennedy and may not have been in control of his own actions. They recalled a case in Copenhagen, in 1951, where a man had been trained to go into a trance at the sight of the letter X. He would then rob a bank and kill anyone who tried to stop him. Had Sirhan been psychologically induced to perform assassinations? If so, who was responsible? Was there a group of conspirators, sophisticated in the latest techniques of mind manipulation, which regularly trained assassins to carry out its dirty work?

Four conspiracy theories were bandied about as possible explanations for the crime. First, there were many people who believed that Sirhan may have had connections with el-Fatah, the Palestinian terrorist organization responsible for many acts of violence in the Middle East and Europe. Sirhan's own pro-Arab and anti-Jewish sympathies linked him with el-Fatah, but there was another, more direct connection. Michael Mc-Cowan, a former Los Angeles policeman, was the chief investigator for the team of lawyers who were to defend Sirhan. McCowan, according to this conspiracy theory, was closely tied with a group of Arabs known as the "Forty Thieves," who had been involved in a land fraud scheme in the San Fernando Valley in 1962. The Forty Thieves, it was believed, were actually an American branch of el-Fatah. It was they who hired Sirhan to kill Kennedy, because Kennedy was a strong supporter of Israel. After the assassination, they had placed McCowan with Sirhan's lawyers to keep an eye on him and to see that he did not reveal the existence of the conspiracy.

A second theory linked Sirhan with organized crime and certain unnamed "oil interests." According to this view, the Mafia hired Sirhan to kill Kennedy and then asked Russell Parsons, a lawyer, to defend him. Parsons was said to have had numerous connections with organized crime and to have defended several leading underworld figures. Moreover, Parsons himself had been investigated by Bobby Kennedy years earlier, when Kennedy was counsel for the Senate Rackets Committee. Parsons had reason to dislike Kennedy and the Mafia had long wanted Kennedy dead because of his threat to destroy organized crime if he became President.

This theory grew more complicated as its supporters delved more deeply into the chain of relationships they had discovered. Eugene Hale Brading, mentioned earlier in connection with President Kennedy's assassination, was known to have connections with the Mafia and with conservative "oil interests" in southern California. In addition, Brading used the same accountant as a prominent Los Angeles businessman who was connected with the Forty Thieves, the suspected el-Fatah front. But most ominous of all was the fact that he had been arrested near Dealey Plaza the day of President Kennedy's assassination, then released after questioning. Had Eugene Hale Brading masterminded the use of Sirhan as an assassin? Was Brading involved in the murders of both Kennedy brothers? Was he the common denominator linking the Mafia, the "oil interests," and the Arabs—all groups that had reason to want Robert Kennedy dead?

A third conspiracy theory pointed to the CIA. As we have seen, some critics had long suspected that the CIA was somehow responsible for the assassination of John Kennedy. Now, a writer who was working on a book on Oswald's connections with the CIA came forward to announce that he had uncovered information proving that the agency was involved in the murder of Robert Kennedy. The writer said that he was not free to disclose the source of his information, but that this source had told him the CIA wanted Kennedy dead because they feared that as President he might launch an investigation into his brother's assassination and discover the role the CIA had played in Dallas.

The fourth conspiracy theory detected Communist participation in the assassination. Sirhan's diary made his leftist sympathies clear. The May 18, 1968, entry, for instance, read: "A list of grievance against US. and its facade of Freedom and Justice for all . . . Freedom is but an imagenary and an elusive concept granted the American, sheep like bourgeois masses, by their selfish . . . overlords. I firmly support the communist cause and its people—wether Russian, Chinese, Albanians, Hungarians or whoever . . . America will soon face a downfall so abysmal, that she will never recover from it."

Moreover, one of Sirhan's closest friends, Walter Crowe, was a member of the Youth Section of the Southern California District of the Communist party. Sirhan and Crowe were known to have discussed politics together on several occasions, the last time as recently as two weeks before the assassination. Had Crowe been ordered by his superiors in the party to find an assassin? Had he chosen Sirhan as a likely candidate and planted the idea in his friend's mind?

In order to look into these questions and others surrounding the death of Robert Kennedy, the Los Angeles Police Department established a group called "Special Unit Senator." Special Unit Senator was made up of the best detectives and investigators Los Angeles had to offer. It was ordered to come up with every possible piece of evidence that could be uncovered. The unit was divided into two sections. The first section was ordered to assist the prosecution and to supply the proof that would help convict Sirhan of murder. The second was to concentrate solely on the question of conspiracy and to check out all leads suggesting that Sirhan had worked with others or had been hired to kill Robert Kennedy.

Sirhan's trial began on January 7, 1969, seven months after the assassination. The case against him was overwhelming. DeWayne Wolfer, a professional criminologist, testified that a bullet taken from Kennedy's body had come from Sirhan's gun. Numerous witnesses were able to identify Sirhan as the man they had seen kill Kennedy at close range. Even Sirhan admitted he had fired the shots. His lawyers concentrated their attempts on saving his life, using as grounds Sirhan's "diminished mental capacity" at the time of the assassination. With Sirhan's own confession at hand and with all the evidence against him, the jury found him guilty.

The second division of Special Unit Senator continued to operate throughout the trial and did not complete its investigation until three months after the trial was over. Its work was more difficult and time-consuming than that of the first division. Each of the conspiracy theories mentioned above was thoroughly checked. The second division, for instance, examined lists with more than 76,000 names on them to see if Sirhan had visited shooting ranges where any of the suspected conspirators had been members.

SIRHAN (RIGHT) IS FOUND GUILTY
OF THE MURDER OF ROBERT KENNEDY.

The second division also checked the backgrounds of Michael McCowan and Russell Parsons, to see if they had met with Sirhan prior to the assassination. It probed Sirhan's relationship to the Communist party and questioned his friend who had been a party member. It looked into the possibility that the CIA had been involved in the assassination and investigated the story of the mysterious woman in the polka-dot dress.

But nowhere did the second division find evidence that Sirhan had been part of a conspiracy. On July 25, 1969, it officially declared its investigation to be closed. The enormous amount of material collected by both divisions was organized into ten volumes and entitled *An Investigation Summary of the Senator Robert F. Kennedy Assassination, June 5, 1968*. Two copies of the report were kept by the Los Angeles police and a third was sent to the Attorney General of the United States.

To date, the information contained in the ten volumes has not been released to the general public. Its conclusions, however, were summarized in a one-volume work called *Special Unit Senator*. These conclusions were five in number: (1) Sirhan Sirhan fired the fatal shots that killed Senator Kennedy and wounded five others in the pantry of the Ambassador Hotel. (2) Sirhan fired those shots with the intent to kill Kennedy and the act had been premeditated. (3) Sirhan was not under the influence of drugs or intoxicants at the time of the assassination. (4) Sirhan was legally sane at the time of the incident. And, (5) there was no evidence of conspiracy.

At the time the report was issued, everyone agreed with its conclusions. There seemed to be no reason to doubt the compelling testimony of so many eyewitnesses. After all, Robert Kennedy's assassination, unlike the assassinations of President Kennedy or Martin Luther King, Jr., had been seen at close range by many people. Sirhan Sirhan had been captured at the scene of the crime, unlike Lee Harvey Oswald, who was taken hours later in another part of Dallas, and James Earl Ray, who remained at large for months. Besides, Sirhan said that he had fired the shots. Oswald had maintained his innocence throughout his questioning and Ray had changed his plea from guilty to not guilty.

Slowly, however, cracks began to appear in the case the prosecution and Special Unit Senator had carefully prepared. These cracks were first discussed at length in a documentary film called *The Second Gun,* prepared by Ted Charach, a Canadian journalist who lived in Los Angeles. Charach toured the country with his film, hoping to drum up interest in reopening the case.

Charach's doubts were seconded by William W. Harper, a man who had made criminology his work for thirty-five years. Harper photographed the two principal bullets used as evidence at the trial and studied them closely. One bullet had been taken from Kennedy's body, the other from William Weisel, one of the five wounded bystanders.

According to the prosecution, the two bullets had been fired from the same gun. Harper, however, believed differently. What interested him most was the difference between the rifling angles on the two bullets. Rifling angles, he explained, are marks etched on bullets as they are spun, after firing, by the spiral rifling grooves in the gun barrel. The rifling grooves help stabilize the bullet in flight after it leaves the gun.

Two bullets shot from the same gun will have very similar rifling angles, since they have gone through the same barrel. On the other hand, two bullets fired from separate guns will have different rifling angles. Harper concluded that the difference between the rifling grooves on the two bullets in the Kennedy case was enough to believe they had been fired by two different guns. "It is, therefore, my opinion," he wrote, "that the bullets . . . could not have been fired from the same gun."

Herbert L. MacDonell, the director of the Laboratory for Forensic Science in Corning, New York, agreed with Harper, but took his interpretation one step further. MacDonell saw the differences in rifling angles, but he also noted the difference in the number of cannelures between the two bullets. Cannelures are ridges or rings running around the circumference of a bullet. They are put there during manufacture. What MacDonell noted was that the bullet taken from Senator Kennedy's body had one cannelure, while the one taken from Weisel had two.

The shell casings in Sirhan's gun showed that his bullets had been manufactured by Omark-C.C.I., a company located in Lewiston, Idaho. When MacDonell contacted Omark, he found that the company had never made ammunition with fewer than two cannelures. What this implied was that the bullet taken from Weisel *could* have come from Sirhan's gun, but that the bullet taken from Kennedy *could not*—it had only one cannelure.

MacDonell also said that he had failed to find any individual characteristics on the two bullets that would positively identify them as having come from the same gun. "The overall sharpness of the Kennedy bullet," he said, "suggests that it was fired from a barrel whose rifling was in far better condition than the one from which the Weisel bullet was fired." Thus MacDonell, like Harper, believed that at least two different guns had been fired in the kitchen pantry.

In the course of his research, William Harper discovered a second problem, the same that has bothered other investigators. He found that the bullets that had been used as evidence at the trial had been mislabeled. They had been marked with the serial number H18602, while the serial number of Sirhan's gun had been H53725. This discovery showed a certain amount of carelessness on the part of the prosecution ballistics experts, but it also raised more difficult questions. Had the police made a complete and thorough investigation? Or had they believed that the eyewitness testimony alone was enough to convict Sirhan and so were careless about the other details in the case? Had the police made proper bullet comparisons under laboratory conditions? Or had they assumed that Sirhan's gun had been the only gun in the pantry at the time of the shooting and that bullet-comparison tests were unnecessary?

The next major area of controversy raised by the critics concerned the distance the bullets had been fired from and the number of bullets that had actually been fired. The experts agreed that the bullet that struck Kennedy behind the right ear had to have been fired from a distance of between 1 and 3 inches (2.5 and 7.6 cm). The bullets that hit him in the right armpit also had to have been fired from a distance of between 1 and 6 inches (2.5 and 15 cm).

The problem was that some of the people nearest to Kennedy when he was shot say that the gun never came close enough to the senator to inflict point-blank wounds. One witness placed Sirhan 7 feet (2.1 m) from Kennedy when the shots were fired. Others placed him at varying distances. No one, however, put him close enough to explain wounds that had been made at a distance of from 1 to 6 inches (2.5 to 15 cm).

And how many shots were fired in the pantry? Sirhan shot eight bullets before he was subdued, yet he wounded five people and struck Kennedy four times. Five wounds plus four seems to equal nine bullets. In addition, there were three bullet holes in the ceiling. Where had all these bullets come from? The police responded with the obvious answer. Some of the bullets were responsible for more than one wound. For instance, the bullet that tore Kennedy's shoulder padding may have gone on to wound a bystander or to hit the ceiling. The critics, however, argued that only a careful study of the pantry would reveal the actual routes of the bullets and whether Sirhan had fired all the shots that were fired.

In 1975, a panel of ballistics experts was established to look into the question of the bullets. It concluded that "no substantive or demonstrable evidence" existed that proved beyond a shadow of a doubt that more than one gun had been fired. The rifling angles and cannelures, it added, could not be used to prove conclusively that the bullets had come from different guns. At the same time, the panel did admit that the bullets it examined lacked characteristics that would prove they had come from Sirhan's gun to the exclusion of all other guns in the world.

In other words, the controversy was left unsettled. Some ballistics experts agreed that the bullets had come from two guns. Other experts said there was no reason to doubt they had come from the same gun. As far as the Los Angeles Police Department was concerned, the case had been solved and was closed. The critics, however, continue to insist that three measures be taken. First, they want a detailed study of the bullets, using the latest scientific equipment. Second, they want an investigation of the ceiling panels from the pantry to see if the routes of the bullets can be determined. Finally, they ask that the *Summary Report,* those ten volumes of evidence collected by Special Unit Senator, be released to the public. Only then, they say, can we begin to settle the problem of the assassination of Robert Kennedy.

Afterword

In 1976, after years of pressure from the critics and segments of the press, the House of Representatives established a committee to investigate the assassinations of President Kennedy and Martin Luther King, Jr. The assassination of Robert Kennedy was not included in the probe because most members of Congress believed it had been adequately solved. Henry B. Gonzalez, a Congressman from Texas, was appointed chairman of the committee, and Richard Sprague, a Philadelphia attorney, was selected chief counsel. The committee was granted a substantial budget and began to set up its staff.

People throughout America were hopeful that the questions concerning the assassinations would now be laid to rest. But early on the committee members began to spend their time bickering and wrangling about problems little related to the assassinations. Sprague, an aggressive and sometimes arrogant man, challenged the leadership of Gonzalez, the Congressman. In Washington, where the elected officials jealously guard their power and influence, that sort of thing is not done. The dispute between the two men reached fever pitch and Sprague was forced to resign. In the aftermath, Gonzalez was replaced as chairman by Louis Stokes of Ohio. Sprague's job was taken over by G. Robert Blakey, a professor of law from Cornell University.

Thus eventually the controversy quieted down, and the committee pursued its work for many months in secret and without comment to the press.

Then, late in the summer of 1978, public hearings on the investigations began to be held, and many people connected in some way with the Kennedy or King assassination were brought before the committee to testify publicly.

Perhaps the most theatrical of these testimonies was given by James Earl Ray, who still insisted on his innocence but gave no new evidence that could clear him of the crime. In fact, the committee came to the conclusion that Ray had indeed been the assassin—but may have not acted alone. There was some indication that others may have aided him, and those others might have been members of his family.

Less theatrical but more startling and with perhaps even greater implications were the committee's findings on the Kennedy assassination, announced just days before the end of the year and right before the committee was to disband. Testimony by acoustics experts, given on the basis of their having listened carefully to a motorcycle policeman's radio dictabelt recording made at the time of the shooting, showed that there was a 95 percent, or greater, probability that there had indeed been two gunmen that day in Dallas, and that almost without a doubt one of the shots fired had come from the grassy knoll, *in front* of the President's limousine.

The chairman of the committee concluded by saying that the committee had no knowledge of who the second gunman might have been, but that it would turn over all the evidence it had gathered to the Justice Department, whom it hoped would pursue the investigations of both Dr. King's and President Kennedy's deaths.

All this sounds hopeful. But it is more than possible that no new evidence will be turned up by any further investigation and that most of the conclusions reached by all three original investigations will stand. This is so partly because in each assassination the evidence still points to the accused men—maybe not to them alone, but to them at least.

At the same time, we should not discount the future efforts of the Justice Department and especially the critics, whose determination and conviction have already uncovered much that was unknown and have pointed to new areas for investigation and exploration. In the future, this determination and dedication may well resolve most, if not all, the questions surrounding these three political murders.

One note of pessimism, however, should be sounded before we close. It is an unpleasant fact, but true, that the assassinations of great leaders are rarely solved to everyone's satisfaction. There are still questions about Abraham Lincoln's death and about the murder of Archduke Francis Ferdinand of Austria-Hungary, whose assassination triggered World War I. Like those assassinations, the assassinations we have discussed in this book may well be disputed for many years with no final resolution.

Suggested Readings

CHAPTER ONE. Two books give long, detailed accounts of what happened in Dallas between November 22 and 24, 1963: William Manchester's *The Death of a President* (New York: Harper & Row, 1967) and Jim Bishop's *The Day Kennedy Was Shot* (New York: Funk & Wagnalls, 1968). Manchester has also written a biography of President Kennedy. Both authors conclude that Oswald was the lone assassin.

CHAPTER TWO. The findings of the Warren Commission are summarized in the *Report of the President's Commission on the Assassination of President Kennedy* (Washington, D.C.: Government Printing Office, 1964). For the determined investigator, there are the twenty-six volumes of evidence published along with the *Report*. These volumes are available in many libraries.

Three books have ably defended the conclusions of the Warren Commission: John Sparrow's *After the Assassination* (New York: Chilmark Press, 1967); Albert H. Newman's *The Assassination of John F. Kennedy: The Reasons Why* (New York: Potter, 1970); and David Belin's *November 22, 1963: You Are the Jury* (New York: Quadrangle, 1973). Belin was an assistant counsel for the Warren Commission.

The background and personality of Lee Harvey Oswald are discussed in Gerald Ford and John R. Stiles' *Portrait of the Assassin* (New York: Simon and Schuster, 1965) and Priscilla J. McMillan's *Marina and Lee* (New York: Harper & Row, 1977). McMillan's book is excellent. She interviewed Oswald in Moscow at the time of his defection to the Soviet Union and later, after the assassination, got to know Marina, Oswald's widow. Both Ford and McMillan argue that Oswald was the lone assassin.

Also interesting is the description of Oswald offered by his brother in Robert L. Oswald, *Lee: A Portrait of Lee Harvey Oswald* (New York: Coward-McCann, 1967). Garry Wills' and Ovid Demaris' *Jack Ruby* (New York: New American Library, 1968) is the best portrait of Ruby and his unusual past.

CHAPTER THREE AND CHAPTER FOUR. The following books present the best arguments made by the critics: Mark Lane, *Rush to Judgment* (New York: Dell, 1975); Harold Weisberg, *Whitewash: The Report on the Warren Report* (Hyattstown, Md.: Weisberg, 1965) and *Whitewash II: The FBI-Secret Service Coverup* (Hyattstown, Md.: Weisberg, 1966); Edward Jay Epstein, *Inquest: The Warren Commission & The Establishment of Truth* (New York: Viking, 1966); Sylvia Meagher, *Accessories After the Fact: The Warren Commission, the Authorities and the Report* (New York: Random, 1976); and Bernard Fensterwald, Jr., *Coincidence or Conspiracy?* (New York: Zebra Books, 1977). Ms. Meagher is also the author of the important *Subject Index to the Warren Report and Hearings and Exhibits* (New York: Scarecrow Press, 1966), a guide to the twenty-six volumes of material published by the Warren Commission along with its report.

Robert Sam Anson's *They've Killed the President!: The Search for the Murderers of John F. Kennedy* (New York: Bantam, 1975) summarizes the main points made by the critics. Peter Dale Scott's *The Assassinations: Dallas and Beyond—a Guide to Coverups and Investigations* (New York: Random, 1976) contains excerpts from a broad spectrum of critical works. Here one can read in one volume the strongest cases made against the Warren Report.

Interesting, but less important critical works are: Richard Popkin, *The Second Oswald* (New York: Avon, 1966); Josiah Thompson, *Six Seconds in Dallas* (New York: Bernard Geis Associates, 1967); and George O'Toole, *The Assassination Tapes* (New York: Penthouse, 1975). Popkin and Thompson believe that there was more than one assassin at Dealey Plaza. O'Toole, using a new machine which he claims can evaluate vocal stress, examined tapes of Oswald's voice made after his arrest and came to the conclusion that Oswald was telling the truth when he said that he had nothing to do with the assassination.

Edward Jay Epstein's *Legend: The Secret World of Lee Harvey Oswald* (New York: Reader's Digest Press and McGraw-Hill, 1978) provides a new and controversial picture of Oswald. Epstein believes that Oswald received training as a spy during the time he was in Russia and was sent back to the United States as a Soviet agent. Epstein concludes, however, that Oswald was not acting under orders when he shot President Kennedy; his espionage activity was relatively unimportant and the Soviets would never have used him on a mission as significant and grave as the assassination of an American President.

Finally, the reader is warned to stay away from several critical works that this author believes are based on fantasy and wild speculation. This is especially true of Thomas G. Buchanan's *Who Killed Kennedy?* (New York: G. P. Putnam's Sons, 1964) and any of the many works by Joachim Joesten.

CHAPTER FIVE. The story of the strange affair in New Orleans is told in Milton Brener's *The Garrison Case* (New York: Potter, 1969). James Kirkwood's *American Grotesque: An Account of the Clay Shaw–Jim Garrison Affair in the City of New Orleans* (New York: Simon and Schuster, 1970) is excellent. Kirkwood, a novelist, met and befriended Clay Shaw. Also important is Edward Jay Epstein's *Counterplot* (New York: Viking, 1969). Epstein was one of the critics who went to New Orleans to help Garrison.

CHAPTER SIX, CHAPTER SEVEN, AND CHAPTER EIGHT. Three important books argue that Ray was the lone assassin of Dr. Martin Luther King, Jr.: William Bradford Huie's *Did the FBI Kill Martin Luther King?* (Original title: He Slew the Dreamer) (Nashville: Nelson, 1977); Gerold Frank's *An American Death* (New York: Bantam, 1973); and George McMillan's *The Making of an Assassin: The Life of James Earl Ray* (Boston: Little, Brown, 1976).

Questions about King's death have been raised by Harold Weisberg's *Frame-up: The Martin Luther King–James Earl Ray Case* (New York: Outerbridge & Dienstfrey, 1971) and Mark Lane and Dick Gregory's *Code Name "Zorro": The Murder of Martin Luther King, Jr.* (Englewood Cliffs, N.J.: Prentice-Hall, 1977).

CHAPTER NINE AND CHAPTER TEN. Several books discuss the assassination of Robert Kennedy at length. The official investigation is summarized in Robert A. Houghton's *Special Unit Senator: The Investigation of the Assassination of Robert Kennedy* (New York: Random House, 1970). Other important works are Godfrey Jansen's *Why Robert Kennedy Was Killed: The Story of Two Victims* (New York: The Third Press, 1973); Robert Blair Kaiser's *"R.F.K. Must Die!" A History of the Robert Kennedy Assassination and Its Aftermath* (New York: E. P. Dutton, 1970); and Jack Kimbrough, *The Killing of Robert Kennedy (An Assassination Scrapbook)* (Published by Jack Kimbrough, 1972). An interesting, if inadequate biography of Sirhan Sirhan has been written by Aziz Shihab, *Sirhan* (San Antonio: Naylor, 1969).

Finally, the reader may find H. Yazijian and S. Blumenthal's *Government by Gunplay: Assassination Conspiracy Theories from Dallas to Today* (New York: New American Library, 1976) useful. It covers the three assassinations discussed in this book.

Index

Mafia, the, 60–62, 66, 82, 136; possible involvement in assassinations, 62, 69, 153–54

Memphis (Tennessee), 87–103, 105, 120; blacks, 87–91, 93–94, 126–27; King in, 89–103, 113–14; marches, 90–91, *92*, 94; officials, 89–90, 94; Ray in, 114–15; sanitation workers strike, 87–91, 93, 126

Mexico, 21, 38, 114, 115, 123, 128

Militants, black, 90–91, 126–27, 138–39

Missouri State Penitentiary, 109, 110, 114, 130

Motorcade, Dallas, 6–12

National Naval Medical Center (Bethesda, Maryland), 22, 49–51

New Orleans, 35, 70, 71, 76, 81, 106, 115; Oswald in, 21, 36, 38, 58, 59, 71, 75

Nonviolence, doctrine of, 88, 90–91, 93, 97, 126

Organized crime, 60–62, 66–68, 70, 136

Oswald, Lee Harvey, 32–33, 61, 164; accomplice theory, 48, 50, 54, 62, 68, 70, 77; aliases, 15–16, 18, 29–30, 58–59, 71, 72; capture and questioning, 18–19, 21–22, 29–30, 52, 158; case against, 19–21, 29–31, 34–35, 40, 45, 49, 53, 146; and CIA, 62–63, 68, 154; communist activities, 21, 35–36, 38, 40, 56–59, 67–68, 75; defection to Russia, 36–39, 56, 63; link to Shaw, 71, 75, 77–78; as lone assassin, 26, 29, 44, 53, 68; maintains innocence, 19, 21, 23, 51, 62, 158; marksmanship, 34, 40, 45–46, 53; motive, 28, 35–40, 51–54; past, 19–22, 28, 30, 35–40, 52, 62–64. *See also* Assassination, John F. Kennedy; Conspiracy theories, JFK; Cuban exiles; Ruby, Jack; Texas School Book Depository; Tippit, J. D.

Oswald, Marina, 19, *25*, 30, 37–39, 63–64

Parkland Memorial Hospital, 15, 48

Police: Dallas, 12, 15, 20–23, 31, 55, 103; Los Angeles, 147–48, 151–52, 155, 157, 160–61; Memphis, 91, 97, 100–104, 113, 122–23

Poor People's March, 89, 94

Poverty, campaign against, 89–90, 122

Racism, 87–90, 125

"Raoul," 114–15, 117–18, 122, 124–25, 129, 131

Ray, James Earl, 109–111, 113, 116, *119,* 120, 123, 125–26, 128–32; accomplice theory, 122–25, 131; Aliases, 102, 105–106, 111–12, 124–25, 129; case against, 106–107, 109, 115–17, 120, 122, 123, 127–28, 146; flight and capture, 111–12, 114, 116,

About the Author

Stephen Goode is a former member of the history faculty at Rutgers University. He holds degrees in history from Davidson College, the University of Virginia, and Rutgers.

Mr. Goode is at present engaged in research and writing in Washington, D.C. He has authored a number of books for Franklin Watts, the latest being a study of America's military complex entitled *The National Defense System*. Mr. Goode is currently at work on a book for Franklin Watts on the subject of Eurocommunism.